Foundations is flat-out brilliant and necessary. We as parents are starving for resources that actually help us create a home of peace, life, vibrancy, and robust discipleship. This book by Troy and Ruth does that, but even more so. So rich and full of grace, I'll be buying ten and giving them to every parent friend I know!

> —Jefferson Bethke, *New York Times* bestselling author of *Jesus > Religion* and *It's Not What You Think*

Troy and Ruth Simons have faithfully pursued Christlikeness in their parenting, and their examples have been inspiring to us in our motherhood journey. We encourage any parent who is hungry for wisdom and guidance to pick up this book and glean from their wisdom.

> —Emily Jensen and Laura Wifler, cofounders of Risen Motherhood, coauthors of *Risen Motherhood*

Foundations is a biblically rich guide for helping parents pass on their faith to their kids. Ruth and Troy share personal stories from their own family to both encourage and equip others. There is so much wisdom in this book, but I especially appreciate their fresh and inviting writing style. If you want your kids to follow Jesus, *Foundations* is filled with ideas you can put into practice today.

> —Sean McDowell, PhD, professor of apologetics at Biola University, popular speaker, coauthor of *So the Next Generation Will Know*

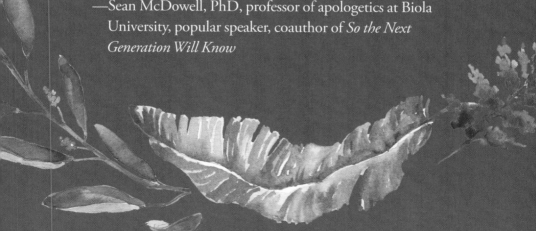

As the mother of seven, I have come to understand this very important truth: You can't pass on what you don't possess. Through the pages of *Foundations*, Troy and Ruth Simons teach parents how to do exactly that—pass on the truths of Scripture to their children. In a world of disengaged parents, the Simonses sound a gospel-centered battle cry: Your kids are worth investing in. Every Christian home needs this important book.

—Heidi St. John, founder of MomStrong International, author of *Becoming MomStrong, Prayers for the Battlefield,* and *Bible Promises for Moms*

Do you ever wonder what people you look up to do to teach their kids about the love of Jesus? When I try to talk to my kids about Jesus, I often find them hanging upside down from the sides of their beds. That's why I'm so grateful for Ruth and Troy Simons. When I first got to know them, I sat around a dinner table listening to how they parent. I had so many questions. *Foundations* is full of the answers! Not only do they help lay a framework for what relationship with God looks like, but they open their front door and allow us into their home to watch how the love of God for them spills into their boys' hearts. The Simons family is a living testimony that knowing Jesus is all about relationship, and this book helps us discover how that relationship can genuinely be passed on to our kids.

—Joshua Straub, PhD, cofounder and president of Famous at Home, coauthor of *What Am I Feeling?*

THIS BOOK BELONGS TO

_____

_____

_____

_____

FOUNDATIONS

RUTH CHOU SIMONS
& TROY SIMONS

HARVEST HOUSE PUBLISHERS
EUGENE, OREGON

To our parents,
who sought to make
love for God and His Word
the foundation of home.

CONTENTS

A Word About Time, and Time in the Word

I remember when our boys were young and one of them was a horrible sleeper for a season, meaning we were up with him several times a night. One morning, flustered and angry over the exhaustion I felt, and excusing myself from any form of discipline or accountability, I looked over and saw Troy getting out of bed to spend time in the Word. I asked, "How can you afford to get up and read your Bible? I'm *so* exhausted and fed up with the lack of sleep!" Troy gently (and without conveying shame or guilt) confessed: "Babe, honestly, I'm not sure if I can afford not to."

To this day, every morning Troy gets up before the sun rises to "get his heart happy in the Lord" (a phrase from his favorite George Mueller quote). And the happiness must be contagious because each of our boys eventually trickles downstairs to join him, starting with our oldest man cub. They start every morning in an embrace, and when I catch it out of the corner of my eye, I get a glimpse of what it's like when we meet with the Lord each day.

We meet with Him, go to the Word, linger in its pages, and pour out our hearts to God in praise and pleading. It's not to merely be more knowledgeable, have more tools, be more literate, or do our duty. Those can't be our only motivation; instead, we meet to enter into our Father's embrace of intimacy, freedom, trust, and character—all of which we can't know apart from *knowing Him* and spending time *with* Him in His Word.

Jen Wilkin says it this way in *Women of the Word*:

> For years I viewed my interaction with the Bible as a debit account: I had a need, so I went to the Bible to withdraw an answer. But we do much better to view our interaction with the Bible as a savings account: I stretch my understanding daily, I deposit what I glean, and I patiently wait for it to accumulate in value, knowing that one day I will need to draw on it.

Relationship will always be a greater motivator than ritual. Relationship is a long-term investment. If you're looking to be more consistent in your Bible time, if you desire for your children to develop a love for God's Word, remind yourself that the Bible is a love letter and a hearty meal at your Father's table. God is already there, waiting for you with arms wide open. We need to come, enjoy the feast and, as parents, show our kids by example where the feasting begins and why He is worthy.

But there's also the matter of the physical time it takes. When is the right time to be in the Word? Where do we find it? Certainly no formula, time frame, or exact method will ensure the spiritual nourishment you need. Troy loves mornings; I don't. But both of us must eat.

Spending time meeting with God and studying His Word may seem natural, easy, and enjoyable for "godly people," but the truth is, it takes work and an investment of time for everyone. Most things we want in life do...

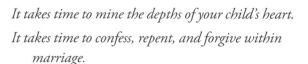

It takes time to mine the depths of your child's heart.

It takes time to confess, repent, and forgive within marriage.

It takes time to listen to the answers to the questions you ask.

It takes time to put as much into a relationship as you want to receive.

It takes time to not just talk about feasting in the Word but to actually do it.

"It takes time" doesn't necessarily mean that change comes slowly (though it may!)—it means that things that matter require a sacrifice of time. Time that you sometimes can't find. Time that seems to slip away. Time that's occupied by the must-dos of life. But if your life is like mine, you can't afford not to make time to be in the Word. Deep relationships, maturity, growth, a disciplined life…these things do not just happen.

The reality is that we demonstrate what is important to us by what we make time for.

If I want real conversations with my kids, I have to make time.

If I want my husband to know my heart, I must prioritize time to make it accessible.

If I want to know my Savior more deeply, I must sow seeds of time in His Word.

The only time I have to spend is the time that is still to come. I can't reassign past moments or reprioritize yesterday's minutes. But I *can* choose what I will value today by how I spend my time. Before the choices are made for me. Before time slips away. Before it's diced and spliced and found insufficient.

Look carefully then how you walk, not as unwise but as wise, making the best use of the time, because the days are evil. Therefore do not be foolish, but understand what the will of the Lord is (Ephesians 5:15-17).

Perhaps you, too, are taking inventory of what you value most...knowing *it's about time.*

Family Worship 101

WHY FAMILY WORSHIP?

Maybe the idea of family worship is new or foreign to you. Maybe you have a preconceived idea or ideal in your mind that it is either forced, cheesy, or unattainable. Sometimes you can give up or not even try when you think you won't be good at or do something perfectly. Here's where we want to encourage you, starting with our *why* of family worship:

- Because despite our good intentions, the words we say to one another in passing can, at best, lack intentionality, and at worst, be misunderstood. Deliberate time together allows for real communication.

- Because not everyone gets to share what they are feeling unless there's a deliberate invitation to do so (especially when you have a large family!).

- Because Deuteronomy 6:7 reminds us to speak of God's Word and to teach it to our children: "Talk of them [God's commands] when you sit in your house, and when you walk by the way, and when you lie down, and when you rise."

- Because gathering together to confess, pray, forgive, and

encourage isn't just for church small groups or Bible studies! It's for the community group in your own home. Worship isn't something we do with a band and a preacher; worship happens any time sinners turn their hearts and hands and lips to praising God, for His glory.

WHAT DO WE DO?

There are two elements that we incorporate into every family worship time: God's Word and prayer.

1. *God's Word.* As we talk about our days or other things that are going on in our family, we're always looking for ways to address what's brought with the truth of God's Word. Even when the Bible doesn't provide a specific answer for a specific dilemma or concern, it always speaks to the principles of the heart.

   When you apply God's truth to your deepest burdens as a family, you'll find that the gospel isn't good news just for salvation but for every moment, great and small, of your daily lives. And don't forget to ask your kids if they know any scriptures that apply to what you're talking about. This teaches them to address their problems by applying what they know of God's Word. You're helping them set up important patterns to fall back on for the rest of their lives.

2. *Prayer.* Pray God's Word, pray for one another, pray for yourself when you're with your family. Humility finds its home in our hearts when we pray.

Beyond these two regular elements in our family worship, it's sometimes clear that something is broken in our family—a place where sin has a foothold and has shown itself in our family relationships. When we're dealing with raw feelings and out-of-control emotions, we need to turn to confession, forgiveness, and reconciliation. When we normalize repentance and forgiveness, we're able to recall together what God's Word says about each situation and work together to reconcile and restore.

- *Confession.* One distinction we make as a family is to focus on *confessing* rather than *accusing*. There's no question that we all have things to confront in someone else, but when we take a posture of confession and ownership, the time is always much more productive.

- *Reconciliation.* Reconciliation is always the goal—with one another and with God. Some children in our household are not yet saved, so they need to see how we wrestle with our own sin and the sin of others, and how we trust Christ for the remedy. No good ever comes from simply venting all that's wrong with relationships or family dynamics. Real change and comfort occur when we submit to the transforming work of Christ through redemption.

FAMILY WORSHIP LOGISTICS

The questions we are asked most often center on how to practically make family worship happen—the logistics. Needless to say, what works for one family won't necessarily suit another. Here are some principles—not formulas—to keep in mind as you form your routine as a family:

- *It doesn't have to be formal or perfect.* Sometimes we gather right after dinner, but most of the time after a long day we just circle up on the floor in someone's bedroom before bed. Don't strive for ideal—just start somewhere. As G.K. Chesterton was known to say: "If a thing is worth doing, it is worth doing badly."

- *Parents: Lead, but involve your kids.* As parents, we lead the time, but we try to draw our children into leading *with* us. We ask them to read scripture and encourage them to ask questions that everyone answers. When you give your children ownership of the time, they'll value it far more.

- *Remember that children learn through observation.* Our kids don't always sit perfectly still, and sometimes they fall asleep while we talk! But don't underestimate what your kids will get from the time simply by observing the people they love, love one another and love God.

- *Make it engaging.* Do what you need to do to get their attention. You don't have to pull out the flannelgraphs, but don't read Scripture monotonously either! Sometimes, when we gather at the breakfast table, we play a dramatic audio Bible reading from *Faith Comes By Hearing.* When they see that you love the Word of God and the practice of prayer, and that you love *them*, they'll be inclined to pay attention.

- *Keep it simple...enough.* We have always used big words—long before the boys could understand them—but we work to help them understand them in context. So, build bridges. Illustrate. Get anecdotal. The exercise of making the difficult passages of God's Word understandable for your children will give you a better understanding as well. Like the Latin proverb *"Docendo discimus"* reminds us, "By teaching, we learn."

- *Make a feast of the stories of Scripture.* Look for ways to connect the stories of the Bible with your own family's story. There is nothing more powerful than informing a child's imagination with the truth of a story when they have critical decisions to make. For example, "This is just like when David had to…" or, "How about when Paul and Silas were singing hymns after being beaten and…"

- *Know your stuff.* This doesn't mean you have to know *everything,* but it does mean you should be prepared for what you're going to talk about. Your knowledge isn't so you can show off but so that your children will see you continuing to "grow in grace."

- *Celebrate, and we mean,* celebrate *the gospel.* Even when your family is struggling through conflict, discouragement, and challenging circumstances—celebrate the kindness of God in Jesus Christ. There is no greater truth for this life!

Just like yours, our family is a work in progress. We are not perfectly consistent with family worship. We can let laziness get the better of us, and sometimes we wait too long to reconcile or deal with hurts. We don't always have the right attitude the first time, and no, our kids aren't always respectful. Just like your family, our family needs Jesus, and we need to see His sanctifying work in each of our lives every day. That's what family worship is all about—drawing close to our Father and one another as we grow in Christ.

Foundational Truths

RUTH

Stradivarius violins are recognized
the world over as unparalleled in sound, quality,
and craftsmanship. I have never seen one in person, but
I hear them spoken of in hushed and reverent tones amid conversations about extraordinary musicians and their instruments.
I can only imagine the warmth and richness of sound that an instrument of that caliber makes. A single line of melody, played with precision and passion on such an exquisite violin, can cause an entire
audience to hold its breath in anticipatory silence.

But imagine that same musical piece, played by the same talented
musician, on an untuned Stradivarius. Depending on how out of
tune the strings are, the melody would not sound as intended. No
matter the quality, rarity, or renown of an instrument, a violin cannot declare the melody it ought without tuning at the hands of its
musician.

The daily practice of worship, of drawing from the well of living
water through the Word of God, is a tuning of heart that causes us to
pour out the praise we were meant to sing with our lives. As the old
hymn says, "Come Thou Fount of every blessing, tune my heart to
sing Thy grace." Those of us who know the melody of redeeming grace

and have been given a transformed heart—an instrument of praise—to worship Jesus in our everyday lives know that sometimes the melody doesn't sound as sweet as it should because we are out of tune. We need our Savior to tune our hearts to His likeness day by day so that we can worship and sing God's grace as we were made to do.

TROY

In the two decades I served as a youth pastor, preaching pastor, and then headmaster of a Christian school, I worked with desperate parents who'd ask repeatedly, "What should I do to lead a family worship time?" "How do I teach my children to love the Lord?" "How do I get my kids to get along at home?" and "What can I do to influence our family culture?"

As a father of six young men, I understand the heart behind these questions. These families want what Ruth and I want: children who become followers of Christ, obey His commands, and fruitfully live out their faith at home and with others. Sometimes we parents want a formula—a magic prescription that will ensure well-behaved, happy kids and a God-honoring home. But there are no formulas or prescriptions that ensure such things. There's only a call to know God and be transformed by Him.

Everything we desire for our families (for ourselves as parents, for our children...for our legacies) begins with heeding the instruction given to the Israelites in Deuteronomy 6 to remember and declare the faithful works of God and to "talk of them when you sit in your house, and when you walk by the way, and when you lie down, and when you rise" (verse 7). The Israelites were told to converse about the ways of God *all the time*, and that's what we need to do because there's no better place to remember and work out the truths of God's Word than with the sinners—um, family members—we live with right at home. Each person in your family or circle of influence (including you) needs the transforming power of God's work in him or her. We as parents, leaders, and influencers don't just teach God's truths diligently because those around us need to hear them, but because we do too.

Family worship isn't the mysterious unicorn of holy parenting. It isn't an unattainable gathering reserved for respectable families with manageable children in clean shirts, hands folded reverently. No, family worship is the intentional tuning of hearts through remembering, praising, believing, honoring, and exalting our holy God as a group of desperate people needing His power to love, forgive, encourage, and exhort one another.

We wrote these 12 resolutions—or family "rules"—not as rules we must work to keep, but as biblical foundations *to rule our hearts*. Whether you choose to use this book for your own growth as a parent, as readings for your family worship, or as a foundational resource within your faith community (the family of believers you walk with), our prayer is that you will find yourself, along with the people in your care, shaped and formed by these truths, intended to change you from the inside out.

By grace,

Ruth and Jim

FOUNDATION 1

LOVE GOD

above all else and with all you've got:

And you shall love the Lord your God with all your heart and with all your soul and with all your mind and with all your strength.

MARK 12:30

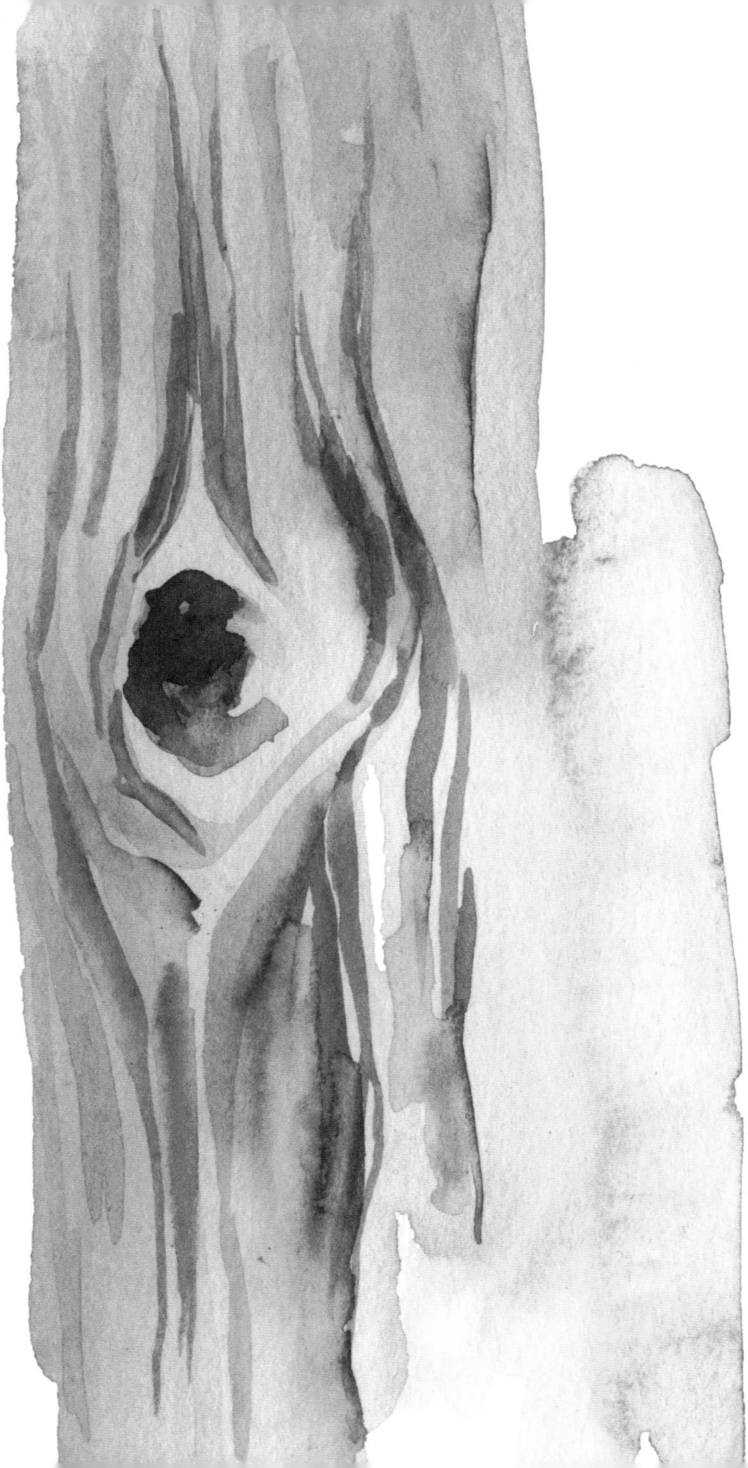

DAY *1*

What Do You Love the Most?

What is it that you love the most? Does something or someone have your heart? Whatever or whoever it is says a lot about who you are. It tells your story, gives hints about your personality, shows how you spend your time. *A mountain bike? A car? A puppy? A girlfriend? Gymnastics?*

When you really love something, you think about it all the time! You can't help but talk about it. *This is the best burger in the world. You have to try it!* That thing you love is so all-consuming it changes the way you live.

We were made to be changed by the love of our Creator God. A relationship with God is not like any other relationship, and His love is unlike other kinds of love. We were made to be so overwhelmed by His love that we love Him most in return. God tells His children to "love the Lord your God with all your heart and with all your soul and with all your strength" (Deuteronomy 6:5 NIV).

What we love most affects everything else we do. If we love our own comfort most, we will do everything we can to make ourselves happy. If we love money and things, we will live with a growing fear of losing it all. If we love to be praised, we will value popularity and fame. God wanted His people, the Israelites, to know His love and to love Him in return with every part of their lives. He knew that loving Him most—with their heart, soul, mind, and strength—would change the way they went about their daily tasks by turning their attention from physical circumstances to the faithful God who provided for them in those circumstances. God invites us, His children, into that bond of love as well.

If we love God more than anything else, we will be shaped by His love for us. That's why God told His people to teach these things diligently to their children and not forget them. Do you see? What makes your heart beat *fast* will determine what your heart beats *for*. So be careful what you love.

TO DWELL ON:

We are shaped by what we love the most.

TO DISCUSS:

1. What do you love the most?
2. How has the love for that thing or person or interest changed who you are in good ways (or not-so-good ways)?

TO MEMORIZE:

> Love the LORD your God with all your heart and
> with all your soul and with all your strength.
>
> DEUTERONOMY 6:5 (NIV)

DAY *2*

Because He First Loved Us

From the first moment a baby enters the world, she is fed, clothed, and protected. She is given a name and becomes part of a family. She knows love from the moment she's welcomed into her mother's arms. Her sense of security and trust begins with her relationship with her parents.

"Everything I have is yours," a dad says to his newborn, "because you are mine." This is how we learn how to love—by receiving love.

How did the disciples know how to love other people after Jesus' death and resurrection? They followed His example. The disciples watched Jesus care for the sick, feed the multitudes, and love the unlovely. They saw Him punished on the cross for their sin so that they might be saved—the ultimate act of love. John was a witness to these acts of love and not only recorded them for his readers, but also shared how we too can respond to that love: "We love because he first loved us" (1 John 4:19).

In the same way that a baby is helpless to give love apart from first being shown love, we would be unable to love God at all if He hadn't loved us first. And just as a child knows the love of her parent by spending time with her mom or dad, we grow in our love for others when we grow in our love for the Lord.

Do you have a friend who is hard to love? Do you lack patience and love for a brother or sister who isn't patient with you? Do you know you're supposed to be loving but don't really know how to start?

Start by remembering God's love for you. Follow His example.

Give what has been given to you. Imitate Him. We love because He loved us first.

TO DWELL ON:

We can love because God loved us first.

TO DISCUSS:

1. Share one thing you've learned to do because of a parent's example.
2. How can you follow Christ's example in loving that friend who is hard to love?

TO MEMORIZE:

We love because he first loved us.

1 JOHN 4:19

DAY 3
After Our Hearts

The church in the ancient city of Ephesus did all the right things. The people there worked hard, pressed on faithfully, and accurately taught the Scriptures. This was a respectable church that looked good, acted good, and made good decisions. It seems like the church at Ephesus was practically faultless—they had perseverance, good works, and an impressive track record. But God said to the people of this church: "You have abandoned the love you had at first" (Revelation 2:4).

While these people thought they were pleasing God with all their good works and attention to detail, God wanted their hearts...He wanted their love. The love they had "at first" was not a giddy feeling or fanatical fervor. They genuinely loved God for His forgiveness and rescue from their sins. But as time went on, the Ephesians began to focus on being busy for God, forgetting all the gratitude they once had for His faithfulness—a gratitude that once stirred up love. They were doing all the right things but without being motivated by the love that drew them to trust in Jesus in the first place.

Loving God with everything you have will always require more than maintaining religious routines or following all the rules. God is after your heart.

So, check your list: Is loving God with all your heart a task to complete, a rule to follow, or an act of your will instead of an offering of your heart? If so, be honest with yourself and your need to remember the God you love. God isn't satisfied simply with your good behavior, so you shouldn't be either. He wants so much more for and from you—He wants you to know His love…and to remain in it.

TO DWELL ON:

God is after our hearts, not just what we can do for Him.

TO DISCUSS:

1. What are some things you *have* to do? What are some things you *want* to do?

2. In what way can you relate to the church at Ephesus?

TO MEMORIZE:

> This people honors me with their lips,
> but their heart is far from me.
> MATTHEW 15:8

DAY 4

An Undivided Heart

Did you know that it is possible to stand in the northern and southern hemispheres at the same time? Just north of Quito, Ecuador, the equator—the line that separates the northern and southern hemispheres of the earth—crosses a place called Mitad del Mundo (middle of the world). A bright yellow line shows where north meets south, and if you visit, you can stand with one foot in each hemisphere. Closer to home, we might straddle a state line while on a road trip and so stand in two states in one stride. Or we can be inside and outside simultaneously when standing in a doorway. While we can think of many ways to be in two places with our bodies, it's not so easy with our hearts.

The Bible tells us that it's impossible to love God and love the world at the same time. God has "delivered us from the domain of darkness and transferred us to the kingdom of his beloved Son" (Colossians 1:13). We are plucked from one spot and firmly placed in another. When we get married, we say yes to that one person and no other. In the same way, God takes us to be His own exclusively. He wants to be our one and only.

The psalmist David prayed this prayer for an undivided heart:

> Teach me your way, LORD, that I may rely on your faithfulness; give me an undivided heart, that I may fear your

name. I will praise you, Lord my God, with all my heart;
I will glorify your name forever (Psalm 86:11-12 NIV).

David knew how tempting it was to try to have his heart in two places at the same time—to love his way *and* God's way, to love the things of the world *and* the things of God. The Bible says it simply can't be done.

Ask the Lord for His help as David did. To love God as He desires—with all our hearts and no less—we must remember anew that He is the one and only true God who is worthy of our undivided attention.

TO DWELL ON:

We cannot fully love God with a divided heart.

TO DISCUSS:

1. Are you capable of doing multiple things well at the same time? How does one task suffer when your attention is divided?

2. What competes for the space in your heart that should belong only to God?

TO MEMORIZE:

Teach me your way, LORD,
that I may rely on your faithfulness;
give me an undivided heart,
that I may fear your name.
PSALM 86:11 (NIV)

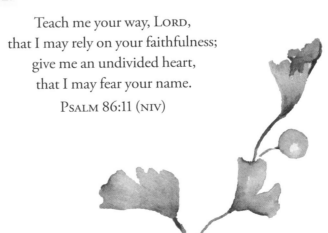

DAY 5

Heart, Soul, Mind, Strength

Have you ever noticed that in the Bible God's greatest displays of love always follow His invitation to trust in impossible ways? God asked Abraham to sacrifice Isaac, the Israelites to head for the Red Sea, Peter to walk on water, a boy to give his entire lunch of loaves and fish, Mary to give birth to Jesus, and Paul to change his name and life path. Whenever God invites His people to be a part of His plan, He asks for what amounts to *everything*. Physically, emotionally, mentally...everything is on the line when God says, "You are Mine."

God even asks for everything when He instructs us in how to love Him: "You shall love the Lord your God with all your heart and with all your soul and with all your mind and with all your strength" (Mark 12:30).

Heart, soul, mind, and strength. Let's look at this some more. Does it feel overwhelming to you? It should! How do we love God with all our heart, all our soul, all our mind, and all our strength? If all means *all*, this instruction feels impossible! So how can we possibly love God above all else and with all we have?

The answer is found in this: "What the law was powerless to do because it was weakened by the flesh, God did by sending his own Son" (Romans 8:3 NIV).

Sin made it impossible for us to achieve what God's perfect standard required, so God sent Jesus to meet that requirement for us. Sin caused brokenness, and in that disrepair we were unable to love Him with whole hearts...with *all* of our hearts. The good news of the gospel is that Jesus remakes the whole person—heart, mind, soul, and strength—so that when we trust Him to fix our brokenness, we become completely whole and wholly able to live with Him forever.

TO DWELL ON:

God wants us to love Him with everything and makes it possible for us to do so.

TO DISCUSS:

1. What stories in Scripture can you think of where God required total trust in everything?

2. What is one way you can love God with all of your heart? Your mind? Your soul? Your strength?

TO MEMORIZE:

> You shall love the Lord your God
> with all your heart and with all your soul and
> with all your mind and with all your strength.
>
> Mark 12:30

FOUNDATION 2

HATE SIN

especially your own.

Let love be genuine.
Abhor what is evil:
hold fast to what is good.

ROMANS 12:9

DAY 1

Everyone's Got Symptoms

If you woke up with a headache and a fever and couldn't keep your breakfast down, you'd certainly conclude that you were sick. Those symptoms are unmistakable signs that you have an unwanted stomach bug or virus. Symptoms can tell us a lot about what's going on inside of us. When it comes to sin, there are symptoms too. Some are obvious, like telling lies or yelling, but some—like wanting our own way—are subtle. One thing we all know for sure is how to please ourselves. We are easily in tune with what we like and don't like, and our default is to put ourselves first. Thinking of our own needs comes naturally, and while it is not sin to take care of ourselves, it's certainly sin when we are ruled by our desire for our own way.

Sin is failing to believe God's rules are best and choosing to live by our own rules instead. God gave Adam and Eve the freedom to eat from any tree in the garden except one. He told them they were not to eat from the tree of the knowledge of good and evil. If you're familiar with the story, you know they didn't choose to obey God. They chose their own way, and ever since then people have made the same choice to rule themselves rather than be ruled by God.

Some of the symptoms of our sinfulness are visible, but the actual weight of our sin can be hard to see from the outside. Have you ever covered up a lie with more lies? Have you talked badly about someone behind their back but pretended to be friendly in person? You see, we hide many of sin's worst symptoms, acting out our best self for others to see. Some symptoms are hidden even from our own eyes until a circumstance reveals them.

In the same way a cough is but an outward sign that something is not well inside, our outward symptoms of sin are a sign of something deeper. If we are to hate our sin, we must recognize it as a much bigger problem than it appears. No one is exempt. No one gets a pass. Though our symptoms may look different, they reveal the bigger problem we each have on the inside. In a world that often downplays the symptoms and makes light of sin, God makes it clear that we are to take sin seriously and trust Jesus for the remedy.

TO DWELL ON:

We need to recognize our real condition as sinners.

TO DISCUSS:

1. When was the last time you were sick with an illness? What were your symptoms?
2. What are some symptoms that reveal the problem of sin in your life?

TO MEMORIZE:

> All have sinned and fall short of the glory of God.
>
> ROMANS 3:23

DAY 2

Sin Hardens the Heart

No one likes to be tricked. Whether it's getting a game that breaks the first time you use it or having someone who pretends to be your best friend talk about you behind your back, you know what it feels like to be fed a lie. Sometimes people call these "rotten apples" or "wolves dressed in sheep's clothing." Whatever you call them, sometimes things can look good on the outside but be dangerous or deadly on the inside.

Sin is one of those things that rarely comes dressed in its true clothing. It appeals to our desires for happiness and satisfaction, but after working its way into our lives, it robs us of the happiness it promised in the first place—like going to a movie that looked fun in the trailer but turned out not to be as good as it seemed. The writer of the book of Hebrews warns against being "hardened by the deceitfulness of sin" (Hebrews 3:13). Sin deceives (or tricks) us into thinking we can enjoy breaking God's rules and then simply move on or manage the sin as we go. But what really happens is that it hardens our hearts.

Have you been tricked by sin? Sin is easy to recognize when someone sins against us. It is easy to hate lying when we've been lied to or hate stealing when someone takes our things. But when it comes to our own sin, we are much less likely to recognize it. We excuse our wrongdoings and downplay our offenses against others. The more we act like our sins are not so bad, the more we believe it. Sin tricks us into thinking that the problem is outside of us when really it is within us.

So how do we keep from being tricked by sin? Sin tricks us by promising things that seem true but are really lies. Just like fake money can seem real unless you are very familiar with the real thing, learning and understanding God's promises is our best defense. The more we study what's true, the more readily we can spot a counterfeit.

TO DWELL ON:

Know God's promises so you won't be deceived by sin.

TO DISCUSS:

1. What are some products you've seen or bought that didn't do what they promised?
2. What are some ways sin tricks us?

TO MEMORIZE:

> But I say, walk by the Spirit, and you will
> not gratify the desires of the flesh.
>
> GALATIANS 5:16

DAY 3
It Starts Small

Most of us have known someone who's fought cancer. The very mention of the word brings an immediate chill because we recognize how serious cancer can be. Even less dangerous cancers get our full attention because they rarely stay small. Cancer can spread, taking over healthy cells and devastating them. We take cancer seriously but so often ignore the danger of sin.

Have you ever told a lie to cover something up and gotten away with it? The next time it's easier to lie again. You've opened the door to dishonesty. Before you know it, you are telling bigger lies to cover for the smaller ones. Lies become a cancer that grows and overtakes your life.

Consider what the apostle Peter warns in his first letter: "Dear friends, I warn you as 'temporary residents and foreigners' to keep away from worldly desires that wage war against your very souls" (1 Peter 2:11 NLT).

Peter wanted believers to remember that they did not belong to this world—they were just journeying through. Notice the picture he paints for them of what it's like to let sin tag along on the journey. It's like war against the soul. Just like cancer wages war on the body, sin wages war on our soul.

Sin is a persistent enemy that we must constantly fight. Great English theologian John Owen said it this way: "Be killing sin, or it will be killing you."

This doesn't mean that we can outsmart or outrun temptation or

Hate Sin, Especially Your Own

our sinful nature. It means that because of Jesus, we have all that we need to resist sin's natural path of destruction. Where sin eventually leads to spiritual death, salvation in Jesus leads to eternal life. We can't beat sin by our own strength and in our own power; we must fight sin with the power of God's forgiveness and redeeming grace. Our Savior overcame sin and death!

> The sting of death is sin, and the power of sin is the law.
> But thanks be to God! He gives us the victory through
> our Lord Jesus Christ (1 Corinthians 15:56-57 NIV).

TO DWELL ON:

Actively fight against sin by asking God to strengthen you in temptation and by trusting Jesus' victory over sin's power.

TO DISCUSS:

1. Do you know someone who's battled cancer? What are some characteristics of his or her disease?

2. Can you think of an example when a small compromise became an overpowering sin?

TO MEMORIZE:

> Keep your heart with all vigilance,
> for from it flow the springs of life.
> PROVERBS 4:23

DAY 4

Love Is Stronger

Have you ever felt so stuffed after a meal that you couldn't think about food at all? You may have been hungry when you sat down at the table, but by the time you'd eaten the turkey, mashed potatoes and gravy, rolls with butter, green bean casserole, Jell-O salad, deviled eggs, Grandma's creamed corn casserole, and homemade cranberry sauce, you really couldn't think about dessert. (Who are we kidding? There's always room for pumpkin pie after Thanksgiving dinner!) The point is, when we are fully satisfied, even the most tempting and decadent treats appear unappetizing...and possibly even disgusting.

The apostle Paul tells us, "Love must be sincere. Hate what is evil; cling to what is good" (Romans 12:9 NIV). When it comes to the Christian life, Paul knew that believers couldn't just hate sin but must cling to their love of Christ. When we love, we turn away from sin because we're focusing on Jesus. If we spend our efforts loving God with all we have, we will naturally hate anything that comes in the way of our love. The more we love what is good and true, the more we will find sin distasteful.

Proverbs 27:7 gives us a perfect picture of this principle: "One who is full loathes honey, but to one who is hungry everything bitter is sweet." We are safest when we believe that everything we need is given to us by Jesus. We are in danger when we are not enjoying God's

45   Hate Sin, Especially Your Own

goodness because then even the bitterness of sin can seem sweet. Jesus is the Living Water who perfectly quenches our thirst. He is the Bread of Life who completely satisfies our hunger. We can fight our sin best when we are satisfied in Him.

TO DWELL ON:

Loving Jesus makes us hate sin.

TO DISCUSS:

1. What is something you say you "hate"? Is it a good thing to despise?
2. What is one way that loving Jesus can make you turn your back on sin?

TO MEMORIZE:

Love must be sincere.
Hate what is evil; cling to what is good.
Romans 12:9 (NIV)

DAY 5

Avoid Wandering, Intentionally

A wise martial arts teacher once asked a student if he knew the most effective way to block a kick. The student thought about the various blocks he had learned, uncertain how to answer. Before the student could venture a guess, the teacher wisely said, "The best block is to not be there." In the fight against sin and temptation, the best defense is to not be in a place of temptation in the first place. The life of King David can illustrate this for us.

King David of Israel was one of the most amazing men of God in the Bible. He wrote many psalms, and he meditated deeply on God. He led the nation of Israel to conquer its enemies and have peace and great prosperity in the land. Not bad for a kid who started out as a shepherd. But he almost lost everything, and it began with a walk on the roof of his palace. The Scriptures tell us that when he should have been out with his army, he sent his friend instead and stayed home (2 Samuel 11:1-5). David then took a walk on his roof one afternoon, saw his friend's wife, Bathsheba, and wanted her to be his own wife. That set things in motion that would nearly destroy him and his family. He killed his friend and married Bathsheba.

Our fight against sin is a daily, ongoing battle, and though we cannot know where every attack will come from, we can recognize our weaknesses and patterns. There are places we should not go, people we should not hang out with, and activities we shouldn't participate in. Making some types of changes in your life will be easier than making others. Some adjustments may be very hard. But whatever it

Hate Sin, Especially Your Own

takes, we must follow David's wisdom in Psalm 16:8: "I have set the LORD always before me; because he is at my right hand, I shall not be shaken."

TO DWELL ON:

Follow Jesus and you will not easily wander into temptation.

TO DISCUSS:

1. How can you fight sin by wisely avoiding temptation?
2. How does obeying Jesus keep you from wandering into temptation?

TO MEMORIZE:

> Watch and pray that you may not enter
> into temptation. The spirit indeed
> is willing, but the flesh is weak.
> MATTHEW 26:41

FOUNDATION 3

HIDE THE WORD
IN YOUR HEART
to live by it.

Let the word of Christ dwell in you richly,
teaching and admonishing one another in all wisdom,
singing psalms and hymns and spiritual songs,
with thankfulness in your hearts to God.

COLOSSIANS 3:16

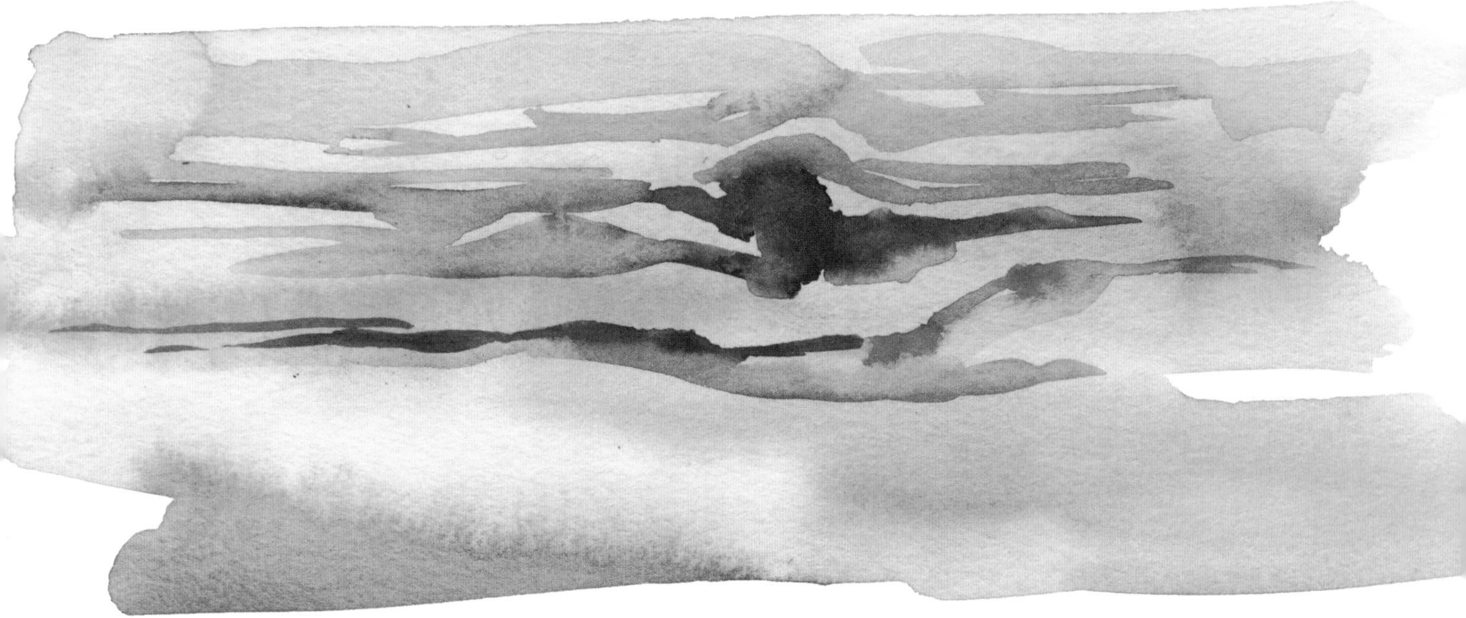

DAY *1*

One Thing to Know

What is the most important thing you can know? *Your address? Your mother's maiden name? Your multiplication tables? A life skill that you can use to make a living?* Think about *Jeopardy*—a game show that leaves your head spinning at the knowledge and facts known by its contestants. For example, do you know the question to this answer: "It's the only U.S. island allowed to use a possessive apostrophe by the U.S. Board on Geographic Names."*

(Give up? The question: *What is Martha's Vineyard?* Who knew?)

We spend a long time—grade school through college!—grasping skills that make us useful and productive.

We all know someone who's able to rattle off a whole bunch of facts, but Jesus told us the most important thing we can possibly know: "This is eternal life, that they know you, the only true God, and Jesus Christ whom you have sent" (John 17:3).

How can we know an infinite and mighty God? How can we know the Son He sent?

God has made Himself known throughout the Bible, His Word. For thousands of years, God worked through the lives of ordinary people to tell us about Himself and His plan for salvation. He used Moses, a simple shepherd, to lead the people of Israel out of slavery in Egypt. Moses took them to Mount Sinai, where God gave them His

---

* http://www.j-archive.com/showgame.php?game_id=2593

words, including the Ten Commandments and the account of how He made the world (Exodus 20:11)! Many people came after Moses, each used by God to bring more of God's words.

When Jesus walked the earth, He was known by those who lived life with Him and listened to His teachings. We can know Him because some of those who walked with God in Old Testament days wrote down what they saw and heard, and others who walked with Jesus in New Testament times recorded the details of His life.

You don't have to be a genius, good at memorization, or super-knowledgeable to know who God is and what He wants for us and from us. It's all in His Word!

> "Let not the wise boast of their wisdom or the strong boast of their strength or the rich boast of their riches, but let the one who boasts boast about this: that they have the understanding to know me, that I am the LORD, who exercises kindness, justice and righteousness on earth, for in these I delight," declares the LORD (Jeremiah 9:23-24 NIV).

The Bible tells us all about God's character and His plan from beginning to end. Through it we can know God and the eternal life He offers us in Jesus. That is *the* story of the Word of God—the love story of God's rescue through Jesus.

TO DWELL ON:

God wants us to know Him through His Word.

TO DISCUSS:

1. Share a fact that you recently learned.
2. What's your favorite thing you've learned about God from the Bible?

TO MEMORIZE:

"Let not the wise boast of their
wisdom or the strong boast of
their strength or the rich boast of
their riches, but let the one who
boasts boast about this: that they have
the understanding to know me,
that I am the LORD, who exercises
kindness, justice and righteousness on
earth, for in these I delight," declares the LORD.

JEREMIAH 9:23-24

DAY 2

Store Up the Word

Have you ever tried to hum a song when another one is playing in your headphones? It's hard to do. Why? Because in that moment, your mind and ears are filled with the lyrics, melody, and rhythm of the song that is coming through your phone or device. You are *filled up* and consumed with the music you're listening to.

That's how it is with our hearts and our habits. When the psalmist who penned Psalm 119 desired to walk in obedience and not sin against God, he didn't ask God to just keep him from sinning. He didn't merely ask for wisdom or for removal of temptation but asked God to *fill him up* with His commands—the Word of God: "With my whole heart I seek you; let me not wander from your commandments! I have stored up your word in my heart, that I might not sin against you" (Psalm 119:10-11).

You see, just as it's difficult to sing the lyrics to a song while listening to another, so a heart filled up with the Word of God runs out of space to sin against Him. Even though as sinners we will always feel tempted to do things our own way without God's help or wisdom, God's grace makes it possible for us to be changed through the content of our hearts. When our hearts become the storehouses for the Word of God—God's laws, commands, and story of redemption—we become living, breathing, walking vessels carrying the truth of God's wisdom and plan...abiding in Him. "No one who abides in him keeps on sinning; no one who keeps on sinning has either seen him or known him" (1 John 3:6).

Abiding is an active choice to continue, to stand your ground, to keep on keeping on. When we abide in Him, we stay affixed to Christ and remain filled up in His Word. We don't let go.

God's Word is not a magic pill that keeps us from sinning. Instead, when we store it up in our hearts, it floods us with truth, filling us up with the gospel's good news melody—so much so that it's the one song we sing.

TO DWELL ON:

Be so filled up with the sweet melody of the Word of God that there is no room for sin.

TO DISCUSS:

1. Think of a time when you were too full to eat something you really loved. What was that like?

2. How has loving Jesus and His Word caused you to resist sin?

TO MEMORIZE:

> I have stored up your word in my heart, that
> I might not sin against you.
>
> Psalm 119:11

DAY 3
Light for Our Path

You don't have to be a camping
expert to know that you must have a lantern when camping in the woods. There's
no darker night than one after the campfire
has died down deep in the mountains. Without a
lantern, making it back to your tent could be a challenging experience. What are those noises you hear? What if
you end up in someone else's tent instead of your own? Invest
in a good lantern—trust me.

God's Word is compared to a lamp and a light. We're told
in Psalm 119:105, "Your word is a lamp to my feet and a light to
my path." It illuminates our path and lights our way. It shines on
God's purposes and plans for His creation. It declares the greatness
of God so that we can see Him, instead of our frustrating circumstances, clearly.

Knowing who God is and how He loves us changes the way and
direction we walk. It impacts our very steps.

So, perhaps you are asking God's direction for a big decision or a
small one. Maybe you're deciding what school to go to, which soccer team to join, how to respond to an unkind classmate, or where
to move to as a family. God's Word directs our steps and lights our
paths when we turn to His wisdom instead and lean on Him for
understanding.

Trust in the LORD with all your heart,
and do not lean on your own understanding.
In all your ways acknowledge him,
and he will make straight your paths (Proverbs 3:5-6).

TO DWELL ON:

Go to the Word of God for wisdom and direction.

TO DISCUSS:

1. What is one thing you wish you had clear directions about right now?

2. How does Proverbs 3:5-6 encourage you as you seek which way to go?

TO MEMORIZE:

Your word is a lamp to my feet and a light to my path.

PSALM 119:105

DAY 4

The Word Pierces Us

Anyone who's played the popular game Operation chuckles at the stressful buzzing sound that signals an unsuccessful removal of a wishbone, funny bone, or spare rib with tweezers. The game tests some hand-eye coordination, but not much else by way of anatomy or surgical procedures (thankfully). You might be able to connect (or disconnect) the ankle bone to the knee bone, or remove a broken heart, but in real life, diagnosing what's really going on inside and separating the good from the bad is much more difficult.

When you're sick or injured, doctors can help to fix broken bones, heal diseases, and connect joints that aren't working properly. But we don't have only physical problems—we have spiritual brokenness too. We need God's Word to help us properly diagnose what's wrong with our hearts.

That's why the writer of the book of Hebrews reminds us to turn to the Word of God for wisdom, clarity, conviction, and discernment:

> The word of God is living and active, sharper than any two-edged sword, piercing to the division of soul and of spirit, of joints and of marrow, and discerning the thoughts and intentions of the heart (Hebrews 4:12).

Discernment is the ability to determine what is right and what is wrong, to be able to see what are truths and what are lies. Discernment allows us to follow wisdom and not just feelings.

Do you usually make decisions by how you feel? The Bible warns us to not "follow our heart" just because it's popular or easy. Why? Because "the heart is deceitful above all things, and desperately sick; who can understand it?" (Jeremiah 17:9). But God's Word, we're told in Hebrews 4:12, is "living and active...discerning the thoughts and intentions of the heart."

The Bible isn't a rule book to follow—it is the living Word that God has spoken to reveal *His* heart. The Word of God cuts through all the confusing, untruthful thoughts that cloud our judgment and exposes what's really going on beneath the surface. And when it does, we find it's more than a plastic Adam's apple or an ankle in the shape of a wrench that needs to be carefully removed from a board game. God actually *replaces* the ways of our old heart with new desires, motivations, and a new love for Him. God's not talking about a physical heart when He says in Ezekiel: "I will give you a new heart, and a new spirit I will put within you. And I will remove the heart of stone from your flesh and give you a heart of flesh" (Ezekiel 36:26). He's talking about the heart as the center of everything you care about most. *That* is the heart God is after, and He uses Scripture to get ahold of it.

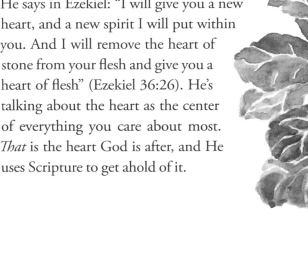

TO DWELL ON:

The Bible reveals what's going on inside of you.

TO DISCUSS:

1. Have you ever seen an X-ray of a part of your body? What surprised you about seeing the "inside" part of you?

2. Do you feel confused about your own feelings and thoughts sometimes? Pray and ask the Lord to replace your feelings with truth from His Word.

TO MEMORIZE:

The word of God is living and active, sharper than any two-edged sword, piercing to the division of soul and of spirit, of joints and of marrow, and discerning the thoughts and intentions of the heart.

HEBREWS 4:12

DAY 5

You Have a Trainer

If you were training in winter for a marathon and owned a treadmill, would you leave it untouched, collecting dust? Would you stop seeing your personal trainer? Would you keep your running shoes tucked away in the closet and wear sandals to train instead? Of course not—we use all the tools we're given to reach the goal we're training for.

But so many believers miss the opportunity to use the resources we've been given when we leave our Bibles on the shelf.

If you look around your house, you'll probably find more than one copy of God's Word lying about on bookshelves, nightstands, and coffee tables. Many Christian homes have multiple versions— Bibles in leather or hardcover, study Bibles, and even Bibles with space for journaling and artwork. We have so many options for reading and studying the Word of God, yet so many of us end up looking elsewhere for help. Listen to what the apostle Paul wrote in a letter to the young man Timothy, whom he discipled in ministry:

> As for you, continue in what you have learned and have firmly believed, knowing from whom you learned it and how from childhood you have been acquainted with the sacred writings, which are able to make you wise for salvation through faith in Christ Jesus. All Scripture is breathed out by God and profitable for teaching, for

reproof, for correction, and for training in righteousness (2 Timothy 3:14-16).

"Able to make you wise," and "profitable for teaching, for reproof, for correction, and for training in righteousness." All of these attributes of Scripture play a part in training us to run the race of faith well. The Bible tells us why God's Word is meant to be used, understood, and treated like a source and resource, not a decoration on the shelf.

In other words, this was Paul saying to Timothy: *Don't stop studying and reminding yourself of what you've learned about who God is and what He's done for you through Jesus. Everything He wants us to know about Him and His love for us has been recorded for us by those whom the Lord used specifically to do the job. Keep on keeping on with those truths at the center of your life. They will make you wise because of Jesus and not because of yourself. They will be your source for anything good you have to teach others. And when you have to say hard things to help someone (including yourself) turn away from sin, the Word of God will keep you in line with what is most useful in helping people change and grow up in godliness.*

The same is true for me and for you, so lace up your sneakers and walk in all that you've been given through the Word of God.

TO DWELL ON:

God's Word will train you up in right ways of thinking and responding.

TO DISCUSS:

1. What is your hobby, and what do you do to train for that sport/interest/hobby?
2. Who told you about Jesus and shared the Word of God with you?

TO MEMORIZE:

All Scripture is breathed out by God and profitable for teaching, for reproof, for correction, and for training in righteousness.
2 Timothy 3:16

FOUNDATION 4

Set your mind where Christ is and ON ALL THAT IS *good and true.*

*If then you have been raised with Christ,
seek the things that are above, where Christ is,
seated at the right hand of God. Set your minds on things
that are above, not on things that are on earth.*

COLOSSIANS 3:1-2

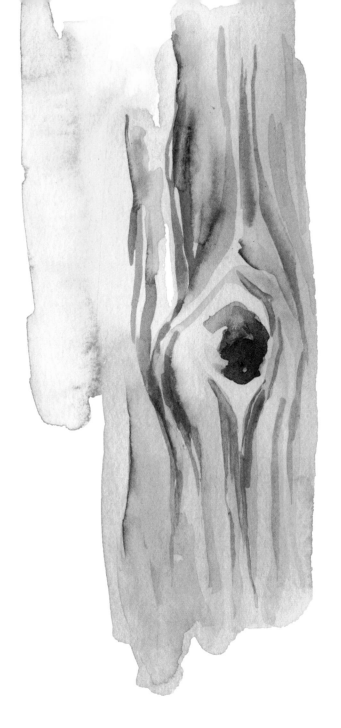

DAY *1*
God Is Capable

Can you imagine the kind of day you would have
if the sun didn't come up? You'd need to do more
than just grab a jacket and a flashlight. It would be so
cold that even all your blankets wouldn't keep you warm. Slowly, the
plants would stop growing, and animals wouldn't be able to find food.
Everything would begin to fall apart, and people wouldn't know what
to do because our very lives depend on the sunrise. Our lives depend
on many things that are outside of our ability to control or orchestrate.
For followers of Jesus, there is great comfort in knowing that God is
the One who can manage everything we can't.

Colossians 1:15-17 tells us that Jesus created everything and holds
all things together:

> He is the image of the invisible God, the firstborn of all
> creation. For by him all things were created, in heaven
> and on earth, visible and invisible, whether thrones or
> dominions or rulers or authorities—all things were
> created through him and for him. And he is before all
> things, and in him all things hold together.

That means that from the smallest particles of matter to the mil-
lions of stars that make up the universe, God is the maker and direc-
tor of everything. It also means that God is in control of governments,
people, and circumstances you find yourself in. That is comforting!

When God reminds us to "set [our] minds on things above"

(Colossians 3:2), He is telling us to trust Him—to remember that He holds all things together, and we do not. We often act as though we are the rulers in our world. What we hear on television and see on the phone or computer gives us the same message—that we control our lives and our circumstances. Sometimes we believe it and work hard to make things just like we think they should be.

The more we think we are in charge, the more we look for ways to fix our problems, manipulate our circumstances, and juggle everything we must do. But in the end, God is the One who holds all things together—directing our steps, planning our course, making a way for us. When we fix our thoughts on Him, we can rest in His direction and provision.

TO DWELL ON:

When we trust that the Lord is capable, we will set our minds on Him and not on our ability to hold everything together.

TO DISCUSS:

1. What do you spend most of your day thinking about?
2. How does knowing God holds all things together set your mind at ease?

TO MEMORIZE:

> He is before all things, and in him all things hold together.
> Colossians 1:17

DAY 2

Stay Focused

Do you know what a ten-mile stare is? It's when your body is present, but your mind is clearly somewhere else. You see it when you're talking to someone in front of you, but he or she seems to be looking past you, somewhere far away. Sometimes we do this ourselves. Maybe it's a daydream, or maybe it's something we are anxious about. It is possible to be one place in our minds and another place in our bodies.

It's not a big deal to daydream sometimes, but being present in the moment is often more important than you realize. If your mind were to wander as a player in the middle of a soccer game, it could cost your team the game. If you daydream in math class, you might miss the instructions and fail a test. Losing focus can be costly, especially in your faith.

The apostle Peter tells us what to do: "Preparing your minds for action, and being sober-minded, set your hope fully on the grace that will be brought to you at the revelation of Jesus Christ" (1 Peter 1:13). Like the coach who tells you to get your head in the game, Peter is telling us that our faith needs to be engaged and ready for action. He was writing to believers who were experiencing trials, persecution, and exile in foreign lands where they couldn't feel at home. He reminded them that it requires focus of mind when their faith is difficult to live out. And just like someone practicing to compete in a sport, the body responds to the mind. If our minds are lazy, our bodies won't be alert and ready. If our minds are engaged and set on hope, as Peter writes, our bodies will be prepared for action in response.

Preparing our minds is a daily work. There are no shortcuts or life hacks to our preparation, but God graciously invites us to come to Him and learn and receive all we need. Our faith grows when we focus on His Word (Romans 10:17) and trust His promises, which enable us to live by His very nature (2 Peter 1:3-4).

TO DWELL ON:

How we focus our minds affects how prepared for action we will be.

TO DISCUSS:

1. Where do you have the hardest time staying focused? In school? Doing homework? Completing chores?
2. What is one way you can focus and prepare your mind at the start of each day?

TO MEMORIZE:

> Therefore, preparing your minds for action, and being sober-minded, set your hope fully on the grace that will be brought to you at the revelation of Jesus Christ.

1 Peter 1:13

DAY 3

Anxious for Nothing

When you learn to drive a car, one of the lessons you will learn is that you shouldn't ride your brake (continually stepping on the brake as you drive downhill). No end of trouble can happen if you do. Riding your brakes all the time will wear them out quickly, but riding them on a steep mountain road may cause them to overheat and quit working altogether. That's a ride that no one wants to take.

Thinking anxious thoughts is like riding our brakes on the steep hills of life. Worry is false security that can comfort and slow down our fears for a while, but in the long run, it leads to disaster. We weren't meant to stop ourselves from going off the road by worrying.

Worry causes us to doubt God's faithfulness. It smothers our faith and robs us of the peace and joy that God promises His children. That is why Paul tells us in Philippians 4:6 not to be anxious for *anything* but to take all our concerns to God in prayer. And the very next verse promises that God will give us peace:

> Do not be anxious about anything, but in everything by prayer and supplication with thanksgiving let your requests be made known to God. And the peace of God, which surpasses all understanding, will guard your hearts and your minds in Christ Jesus (Philippians 4:6-7).

Set Your Mind Where Christ Is and on All That Is Good and True

When we feel anxious or worried, we have a choice. We can focus on that worry, thinking we can control our situation and riding our mental brakes until they fail. Or we can take that worry to God, focusing on Him as He carries us to safety.

TO DWELL ON:

Worry is not believing that God is in control.

TO DISCUSS:

1. What are some things you are worried about right now?
2. Do you worry when you believe that God is in control, or when you feel that you are in control?

TO MEMORIZE:

Do not be anxious about anything, but in everything by prayer and supplication with thanksgiving let your requests be made known to God. And the peace of God, which surpasses all understanding, will guard your hearts and your minds in Christ Jesus.

PHILIPPIANS 4:6-7

DAY 4

Whatever Is

Have you ever considered how many things there are to think about in a day? Work, school, after-school activities, books, phone calls, social media...Text messages can amount to a never-ending conversation. And some people have other entertainment opportunities—Netflix, YouTube, video games, and more. All these things come so fast and easy that we don't stop to consider if all we *are* thinking about is what we *should* be thinking about. If you are what you think, what you choose to think about needs close consideration.

The apostle Paul recognized how important it is to think about the right things. He told the Philippians:

> Whatever is true, whatever is honorable, whatever is just, whatever is pure, whatever is lovely, whatever is commendable, if there is any excellence, if there is anything worthy of praise, think about these things (4:8).

Did you notice that Paul doesn't give us specific things to think about? He doesn't say "yes" to classical music or "no" to corny jokes, "yes" to philosophy or "no" to song lyrics. Paul makes it clear that we aren't to give bits and pieces of our thoughts to the Lord—we are to think about anything and everything that brings Him praise. Every day, all the time, whatever reflects the goodness of God—think about those things!

God wants to transform our minds by conforming them to all

that is true, beautiful, and good—all that is just like Him. It does matter what we think about because action always follows thought. It is not just that we need to stop thinking about certain things. We need to replace our unfruitful or useless thoughts with "anything worthy of praise" thoughts. God has given us no shortage of amazing things to think on—Himself most of all.

TO DWELL ON:

We were made to think on everything that is like Jesus.

TO DISCUSS:

1. What are some things that don't fall into the *whatevers* that Paul instructs us to think about?
2. How is Jesus true, honorable, just, excellent, and worthy of praise?

TO MEMORIZE:

Finally, brothers, whatever is true, whatever is honorable, whatever is just, whatever is pure, whatever is lovely, whatever is commendable, if there is any excellence, if there is anything worthy of praise, think about these things.

PHILIPPIANS 4:8

DAY 5
Prayer

Can you imagine a movie without a soundtrack? The plot may be amazing and the acting superb, but without the musical score, something would not feel quite right. Think how *Star Wars* would look if it opened with the floating words but dead silence. Can you see it in your mind? Without music? Not very inspiring, right? The music is a key part of the story. It grips us and sets the tone for the movie. In a similar way, prayer is a necessity for the life of one who follows Jesus. It's a critical part of setting our minds on Him.

It is possible and even quite common for people to know a great deal about God without knowing Him personally. Going to church and listening to sermons will result in learning much about the Bible if you pay attention and keep at it for a long time, and that is important because we must know about God if we are to follow and obey Him. But we must not stop with just knowing about God. He calls us to know Him in a personal way, and prayer is our personal connection to Him.

In 1 Thessalonians 5:16-18, Paul instructs us to "rejoice always, pray without ceasing, give thanks in all circumstances; for this is the will of God in Christ Jesus for you." Prayer is smack-dab in the middle of "always" and "in *all* circumstances," sandwiched right between the two. God invites us to talk with Him *all the time*. He doesn't get tired of listening to us, and He meets us every time we turn our hearts and our minds to Him in prayer. Turns out, it's God's will for us. He's wired us to continually find joy in all circumstances as we give Him thanks for the way He works in our lives. Prayer helps us see, hear, and agree with our hearts and minds that He is good.

TO DWELL ON:

Prayer is talking with God, setting our hearts and minds to agree with what God is doing in our lives.

TO DISCUSS:

1. Do you talk to God in prayer regularly or only at mealtimes and when you are in need? What are some other times you could pray?

2. What are reasons why you cease (or stop) praying? Is it laziness? Disbelief? Forgetfulness? Ask God to teach you to talk to Him continually.

TO MEMORIZE:

Rejoice always, pray without ceasing, give
thanks in all circumstances; for this is
the will of God in Christ Jesus for you.

1 THESSALONIANS 5:16-18

FOUNDATION 5

BE AN
ENCOURAGER

BUILD EACH OTHER UP.

*Therefore encourage one another and
build one another up, just as you are doing.*

1 THESSALONIANS 5:11

DAY *1*

True Courage

Did you know most of the words we use in the English language come from words that were originally used in another language? Take the word "encourage," for example. It originates from an old French word that conveyed the idea of "putting in courage." That's quite a picture—to fill a vessel up with courage. Can you see it? That's what we do when we encourage others.

But, if we are to be encouragers, we must know what true courage is. How else will we know what to fill others up with? What often passes as encouragement is a far cry from instilling true courage in someone's heart. For instance, it might *feel* good to count the number of likes you get or the positive comments you receive, but does that *fill* you up with true courage? We all like to be around people who say nice things about us. It feels good in the moment when someone says, "You're awesome," but what do we do when we are not awesome—and we know it? We need something more than accolades.

To understand encouragement, it's helpful to recognize where the problems that dishearten us come from. What *dis*courages us? You might immediately think of the unkind classmate at school, your flimsy bank account, or the amount of laundry that still must be done. It may feel as though a change in those areas would encourage you. Turns out, a transformation in circumstance is secondary to a change of heart. Hear what David asked of the Lord in his discouragement:

Hear my cry, O God, listen to my prayer; from the end
of the earth I call to you when my heart is faint. Lead me
to the rock that is higher than I (Psalm 61:1-2).

It is our hearts that grow faint—and it is our hearts that must be
filled up with courage in any circumstance. David doesn't ask God to
change his situation or make him stronger or faster. He simply asks
the Lord to change his heart by taking him to a source bigger than
himself. He asks God to lead him to "the rock that is higher than I."
And who is that rock? It is God Himself!

As Christ-followers, we know God to be our true courage—our
true hope, true power, true wisdom. Therefore, to encourage one
another is to put truth—not counterfeit praise—into our faint (and
sometimes leaky) hearts. We get to fill each other up with true courage!

TO DWELL ON:

True encouragement is to be filled up with truth in Christ.

TO DISCUSS:

1. What is the most encouraging thing someone has said to you
   lately?
2. Where are you lacking courage? What truth of God's Word can
   you put into your heart in place of discouragement? Now speak
   that to someone else!

TO MEMORIZE:

Speak to one another with psalms, hymns, and spiritual
songs. Sing and make music in your hearts to the Lord.

EPHESIANS 5:19 (BSB)

DAY 2

Encourage Daily

Do you play an instrument? Piano, violin, flute, guitar? Learning an instrument is fun and exciting when you first receive your instrument and play a few notes on it. It's fun to imagine yourself a maestro at the piano or a songwriter at your guitar, but all accomplished musicians have one thing in common: They practice. It's safe to say they practice a lot.

Piano teachers often tell their students to practice every single day. Many believe that a little practice every single day is more effective in honing a skill than a few longer sessions of practice between lessons.

There's something about daily practice—the retraining and rehearsing of a skill day by day—that makes the skill second nature. Practice is the difference between defaulting to confidence or feeling desperate and unprepared. So, it's no wonder that the writer of Hebrews frames the work of encouragement in terms of daily practice:

> See to it, brothers and sisters, that none of you has a sinful, unbelieving heart that turns away from the living God. But encourage one another daily, as long as it is called "Today," so that none of you may be hardened by sin's deceitfulness (Hebrews 3:12-13 NIV).

Encourage one another *every day* to believe and remember God. This is the blueprint for defaulting to the truth instead of our feelings.

We must remind each other of God's faithfulness, and we must do so daily—just like practicing the piano or any other skill we want engrained in our routine. We can easily forget God's promises and sometimes His warnings against sin each day. That's why we need to repeat the truth about who Jesus is and what He's done to free us from the bondage of sin—*before, during,* and *after* we wander into lies. When we practice daily encouragement in truth, we learn to default to confidence in Christ instead of desperation in our feelings. We need one another to be steadfast.

Daily starts today.

TO DWELL ON:

Encourage one another every day to choose God instead of sin.

TO DISCUSS:

1. Describe a time you felt most encouraged in the Lord.
2. Whom can you invite to encourage you with truth every day, so you can fight the temptation to sin?

TO MEMORIZE:

> But encourage one another daily,
> as long as it is called "Today,"
> so that none of you may be hardened
> by sin's deceitfulness.
> HEBREWS 3:13 (NIV)

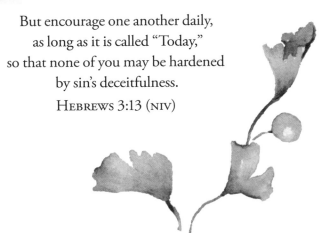

DAY 3

How to Encourage

Have you ever played the game Jenga, where wood blocks are stacked and players carefully remove individual blocks without causing the entire tower of blocks to tumble? The game illustrates a simple principle: Nothing can stand without a firm foundation. Without being strong at its base, a tower will eventually fall.

No wonder the Bible gives explicit instructions for believers not only to encourage each other but to build each other up. Do you know what it means to build someone up? The apostle Paul said:

> You are not in darkness, brothers, for that day to surprise you like a thief. For you are all children of light, children of the day. We are not of the night or of the darkness. So then let us not sleep, as others do, but let us keep awake and be sober. For those who sleep, sleep at night, and those who get drunk, are drunk at night. But since we belong to the day, let us be sober, having put on the breastplate of faith and love, and for a helmet the hope of salvation. For God has not destined us for wrath, but to obtain salvation through our Lord Jesus Christ, who died for us so that whether we are awake or asleep we might live with him. Therefore encourage one another and build one another up, just as you are doing (1 Thessalonians 5:4-11).

Paul's encouragement to the people of this church was for them to remind each other that they were children of light, saved by Jesus and given the armor of God to stay alert and ready as followers of Christ. He instructed them to build each other up in these truths.

When we encourage one another to put on our armor, stand firm, and remember the power of Jesus, we build each other up like a tower or defense that cannot fall.

TO DWELL ON:

It is every believer's responsibility to build others up with truth about what we have in Jesus.

TO DISCUSS:

1. Who is someone who builds you up? How?
2. What are some ways we can build each other up in this family?

TO MEMORIZE:

> Therefore encourage one another and build
> one another up, just as you are doing.
> 1 Thessalonians 5:11

DAY *4*

Encourage When Things Are Hard

You see it on the playground when kids reject other kids. You see it down the street when a neighbor's home is lost in a fire. You hear about it across the globe as people suffer from pain and hunger. People are hurting all around us—at school, at work, on the soccer field, in our home.

As followers of Christ, we are not exempt from pain and hardships. In fact, we're told to expect them. But, in Christ, we have every encouragement through the promises that God has made. When answers cannot be found, His promises still stand and help us persevere. To be an encourager, a bearer of truth, you don't need to know everything. Here are five simple truths from Romans 8:26-39 to help when you want to encourage yourself or someone else who is facing difficulties:

1. *The Spirit helps us in our weakness.* "In the same way, the Spirit helps us in our weakness. We do not know what we ought to pray for, but the Spirit himself intercedes for us through wordless groans" (Romans 8:26 NIV).

2. *God is in control.* "We know that in all things God works for the good of those who love him, who have been called according to his purpose" (Romans 8:28 NIV).

3. *There's no one to fear.* "If God is for us, who can be against us?" (Romans 8:31).

4. *We are already overcomers.* "No, in all these things we are more than conquerors through him who loved us" (Romans 8:37).

5. *Nothing can separate us from the love of God.* "I am convinced that neither death nor life, neither angels nor demons, neither the present nor the future, nor any powers, neither height nor depth, nor anything else in all creation, will be able to separate us from the love of God that is in Christ Jesus our Lord" (Romans 8:38-39 NIV).

TO DWELL ON:

God's love is our encouragement in the middle of hardship.

TO DISCUSS:

1. What is a hard circumstance you're currently experiencing?
2. How does God's love—which we can't be separated from—encourage you right now?

TO MEMORIZE:

I am convinced that neither death nor life, neither angels nor demons, neither the present nor the future, nor any powers, neither height nor depth, nor anything else in all creation, will be able to separate us from the love of God that is in Christ Jesus our Lord.

ROMANS 8:38-39 (NIV)

DAY 5
Quality Time

Have you noticed that when you go to see a great movie, eat a super-delicious meal, or discover a fun new game, you immediately look for an opportunity to share the experience with someone else? You offer to go see that movie again with your friends—just to enjoy it with them. You take your friends to your favorite restaurant the first chance you get. Or you plan a game night and invite people over so that the fun can be shared. We're naturally wired to want to enjoy the best things together, in community.

We need each other—not just to do fun things with or to keep us company, but because we are made to influence one another when we spend time together. The writer of Hebrews encouraged believers not to get lazy about spending quality time together but to worship, to encourage one another, and to build each other up:

> Let us consider how we may spur one another on toward
> love and good deeds, not giving up meeting together,
> as some are in the habit of doing, but encouraging one
> another—and all the more as you see the Day approach-
> ing (Hebrews 10:24-25 NIV).

The writer specifically instructed believers to spend time together encouraging and spurring one another on toward love and good deeds. How important it is for us as the body of Christ to consistently spend time with our church community. And that begins right at home. Are you deliberate about encouraging and spurring on your brother or sister? Your mom or dad? Parents, are you eager to spur your kids on toward love and good deeds by investing in their encouragement through quality time? There are really no shortcuts to encouragement; it takes time and intentionality. When we take seriously the purpose of building one another up, we will think of our time with those around us differently, and by God's grace…invest more wisely.

TO DWELL ON:

Spend time with others to spur them on.

TO DISCUSS:

1. What encourages you most to love others?
2. How can you be more intentional about spending time with other believers—in your home and in your community?

TO MEMORIZE:

Let us consider how we may spur one another on toward love and good deeds, not giving up meeting together, as some are in the habit of doing, but encouraging one another—and all the more as you see the Day approaching.

Hebrews 10:24-25 (NIV)

FOUNDATION 6

give generously

IN WORD, ACTION, AND SUPPLY — THERE IS NOTHING TO LOSE.

He who supplies seed to the sower and bread for food
will supply and multiply your seed for sowing and
increase the harvest of your righteousness.

2 CORINTHIANS 9:10

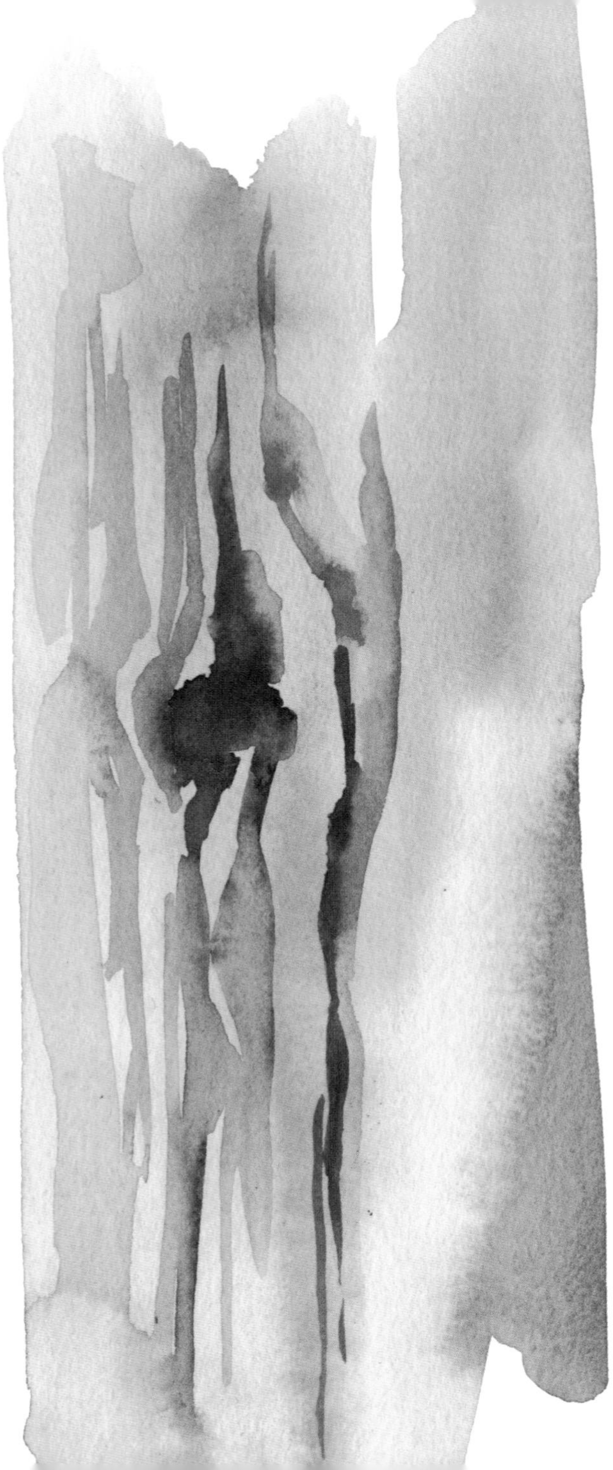

DAY *1*

The Most Generous Giver

Do you experience the four seasons where you live? Does it snow in wintertime? If you've ever lived in or visited mountainous areas in wintertime, you know that winter brings incredible amounts of snow, so much so that the snow on the highest peaks never fully melts even in summer. When spring arrives, another glorious change occurs as snow slowly melts and supplies the mountains with water. Trees put on their leaves, and wildflowers clothe the fields. The transformation goes well beyond just the mountains. Runoff reaches the lower elevations, giving life to the entire region. Everyone benefits, down to the smallest forest creature. The abundance of snowfall in winter affects every season after.

But unlike the mountaintops covered in snow, the lowest place on earth, the Dead Sea in Israel, continually receives water from the Jordan River and underground springs but cannot pass it on. With no outlet for its waters, the Dead Sea is largely lifeless.

The trickle effect of giving generously is a bit like the effect of snowfall on the mountain. The apostle James says, "Every good gift and every perfect gift is from above, coming down from the Father of lights, with whom there is no variation or shadow due to change" (James 1:17). *Every gift!* All that we have is given to us by God out of His goodness. Our very life, our minds, all that makes us who we are has come from the One who created and sustains all things. But

God's generosity isn't wrapped up only in things. His greatest gift is *Himself.* The most generous Giver of all gave His Son, Jesus Christ, to rescue us from sin and death through His own death on a cross. His gift of redemption was the greatest act of generosity because it was the most undeserved gift of grace.

Receiving such a generous gift from the most generous Giver in turn supplies every area of our lives with grace to overflow to others. Not to hold onto, like the Dead Sea, but to give generously—to pour out and "pay it forward"—and to offer to others what has so generously been given to us.

TO DWELL ON:

We can be generous givers when everything we treasure comes from the most generous Giver of all.

TO DISCUSS:

1. What are some of the most favorite gifts you've ever received?
2. Make a list of the blessings you've received in Christ, and talk about how those blessings can bless others.

TO MEMORIZE:

Every good gift and every perfect gift is from above,
coming down from the Father of lights, with whom
there is no variation or shadow due to change.

JAMES 1:17

DAY 2
We Lack Nothing

Why do we write our names on labels of
jackets and on backpacks, water bottles, and
uniforms? So that our belongings don't get misplaced, stolen, or lost at school or on the soccer field, of course. Ownership matters as we manage our belongings, protect our resources,
and use what we have. You know which water bottle belongs to you at
the soccer field because you've put your name on it. But what if *every*
water bottle at the soccer field belonged to you? Every single one used
by every single player? There would be no need to write your name on
each one. Everyone would know that you own *all* the water bottles
and have given them freely for *all* to use.

The Bible tells us that God "owns the cattle on a thousand hills"
(Psalm 50:10). And even more than that, the psalmist says, "The earth is
the LORD's and everything in it, the world and all who live in it" (Psalm
24:1 NIV). God owns *everything*! Our houses, our toys, the food in our
pantries—they're all God's and given by Him for us to use.

If everything belongs to the Lord and is given *by* Him for us to use
for Him, why do we sometimes say things like:

"I could help if I had a bigger allowance."

"I would be a better friend if I had more time."

"I'm not good enough for the job that needs to be done."

"I don't have enough to give to make a difference."

Do you ever think these things, believing that you lack what it takes to give generously? It's so tempting to dig inside our backpacks, handbags, or drawers and think our resources are not enough. But the Bible tells us not to worry about where we will get our food, our shelter, or our clothes because God provides for us:

> I tell you, do not be anxious about your life, what you will eat or what you will drink, nor about your body, what you will put on. Is not life more than food, and the body more than clothing? Look at the birds of the air: they neither sow nor reap nor gather into barns, and yet your heavenly Father feeds them. Are you not of more value than they? (Matthew 6:25-26).

We lack nothing because God supplies everything. When all we truly need is provided by God, we don't need to worry about running out. He owns it all, remember? Giving generously, sharing whatever we've been given, and offering our time and talents is a response to His faithful provision. Start freely counting your blessings, and before you know it, you'll find yourself freely giving them away.

TO DWELL ON:

We lack nothing when everything belongs to our good God.

TO DISCUSS:

1. Do you like to collect things? What is something you own lots of?

2. How can you be more generous with your time, money, or energy with someone in your life?

TO MEMORIZE:

I tell you, do not be anxious about your life, what you will eat or what you will drink, nor about your body, what you will put on. Is not life more than food, and the body more than clothing?

MATTHEW 6:25

DAY 3
Cheerful Generosity

Have you ever received a simple
gift that felt extravagant because of
what it cost the giver? A crocheted blanket? A
homemade meal? A small present purchased
with an allowance saved in a piggy bank? A gener-
ous person is someone who gives when he doesn't have to, gives when
he may not receive anything in return. He shares with others what is
costly for him. Can you think of someone like that in your life?

Generosity is more about sacrifice than about cost. It's a matter of
the heart. A poor person can be generous just as a wealthy person can
be miserly. It's not how much we give, but the attitude with which
we give it. Think about it: We don't call it generosity if it doesn't cost
the giver anything. We call it generosity because the gift is an intentional choice to bless.

That's why the apostle Paul summarized his encouragement to the
Corinthians about purposeful giving like this:

> The point is this: whoever sows sparingly will also reap
> sparingly, and whoever sows bountifully will also reap
> bountifully. Each one must give as he has decided in
> his heart, not reluctantly or under compulsion, for God
> loves a cheerful giver (2 Corinthians 9:6-7).

God sees the heart from which we give our time, money, words,
and resources. He loves it when we give cheerfully! So how do we

offer what we have to others with a happy heart even when it feels inconvenient, costly, or sometimes even unappreciated? How do we become cheerful givers? *We set our aim on pleasing the God who gave generously out of His good pleasure.*

Generosity is *heart-shaping* for the giver as much as it is a *blessing* for the receiver. God uses giving as one way to change our hearts: "Incline my heart to your testimonies, and not to selfish gain!" says the psalmist (Psalm 119:36). The more we delight in the Lord, the more our hearts lean *away* from selfishness and *toward* generosity. What sets us as Christ-followers apart from other people who give generously is purpose. God calls us to be generous as a response to Him—not to look better, feel better, or to make a name for ourselves but to joyfully give to others as He has given to us.

TO DWELL ON:

How we give is more important than how much we give.

TO DISCUSS:

1. Describe a time when giving generously made you happy.
2. In what way can you give your time, words, or resources more generously?

TO MEMORIZE:

God loves a cheerful giver.

2 Corinthians 9:7

DAY 4

Overflowing

You have probably heard the children's rhyme, "Sticks and stones may break my bones, but words can never hurt me." We all know that this simply isn't true. Have you ever been called an unkind name, spoken to rudely, or misrepresented by someone else? If so, you know that words can hurt more than a broken bone.

Call it rude behavior or bad manners, but hurtful and unkind words simply reveal what's on the inside of the person. Words are an overflow of the heart. You can learn a lot about someone by the words he or she speaks when "squeezed" or under pressure. What's on the inside comes out!

But the hope of the gospel is that when we trust Jesus to forgive our sins, He replaces the sinful "natural self" inside of us with "a new creation" (2 Corinthians 5:17) and fills us up with all that is good and true in Christ:

> The good person out of the good treasure of his heart produces good, and the evil person out of his evil treasure produces evil, for out of the abundance of the heart his mouth speaks (Luke 6:45).

Our mouths speak from the content of our hearts. It's like putting money in a bank account—we need to store up truth if we are to speak from overflow. Do you store up truth from God's Word, or from other people's opinions? Are you filled up with grateful reminders of God's faithfulness, or are you dwelling on bitter things? What consumes your heart and mind will, as the verse reminds us, determine the words you speak. Some people say about nutrition, "You are what you eat," but it may be true of our speech as well.

Do you want to be generous in speech and gracious with your words? Just as you might give generously from your abundance of food or clothing, you can only give generously with words when you're abundantly filled up.

TO DWELL ON:

Our words reveal the contents of our hearts.

TO DISCUSS:

1. Has someone said something hurtful to you recently? What did it reveal about that person's heart?

2. What are you most consumed with in your thoughts? How do your words reflect how you are being filled up?

TO MEMORIZE:

> Out of the abundance of the heart his mouth speaks.
>
> Luke 6:45

DAY 5

Nothing Compares

In 1956, a missionary named Jim Elliot was killed by members of the Auca tribe to whom he was ministering in Ecuador. Many of the Aucas later came to know the Lord because of the life and work of Elliot and the other brave men he served with. Jim Elliot's life mirrored his most well-known quote: "He is no fool who gives what he cannot keep to gain that which he cannot lose."

For Jim Elliot, eternal treasure outweighed any earthly wealth, possessions, or desires. He held everything—even his life—with open hands because what mattered most to him (redemption! life in Christ!) could not be taken away from him no matter his circumstances. He had nothing to lose.

Sometimes people say they have nothing to lose when they don't really care. But that's not what Paul had in mind when he wrote to the Philippians:

> Indeed, I count everything as loss because of the surpassing worth of knowing Christ Jesus my Lord. For his sake I have suffered the loss of all things and count them as rubbish, in order that I may gain Christ (Philippians 3:8).

Nothing to lose meant everything to gain for Paul. Paul wasn't indifferent. He was deeply aware of his forever treasure in Christ. He simply had no fear in giving anything and everything away because nothing on earth compared to what he treasured in Jesus.

We too can hold all our possessions with open hands, giving generously with nothing to lose. Just like Paul, we are called to count—or consider—all that we have as second best to having Jesus. We have nothing to lose because God supplies us with the eternally lasting gift of His love, His presence, and His assurance when we put our trust in Him. More than any gift card, fund-raiser, donation, or volunteer work we can offer, the most generous gift we can give is to share the hope of salvation in Jesus with others. Unlike any earthly gain, it is a gift that can't be depleted and cannot be lost.

TO DWELL ON:

You have nothing to lose when you give the good news of Jesus away generously.

TO DISCUSS:

1. Have you ever lost something very valuable to you? What was it? What does that say about knowing Jesus Christ as Lord if Paul calls the loss of all other things worthless?

2. By Jim Elliot's definition, are people generally foolish or wise in our culture today? Why do you think that?

TO MEMORIZE:

Indeed, I count everything as loss because of the surpassing worth of knowing Christ Jesus my Lord. For his sake I have suffered the loss of all things and count them as rubbish, in order that I may gain Christ.

PHILIPPIANS 3:8

FOUNDATION 7

WALK WISELY

that Christ might be visible.

*Walk in wisdom toward outsiders,
making the best use of the time.*

COLOSSIANS 4:5

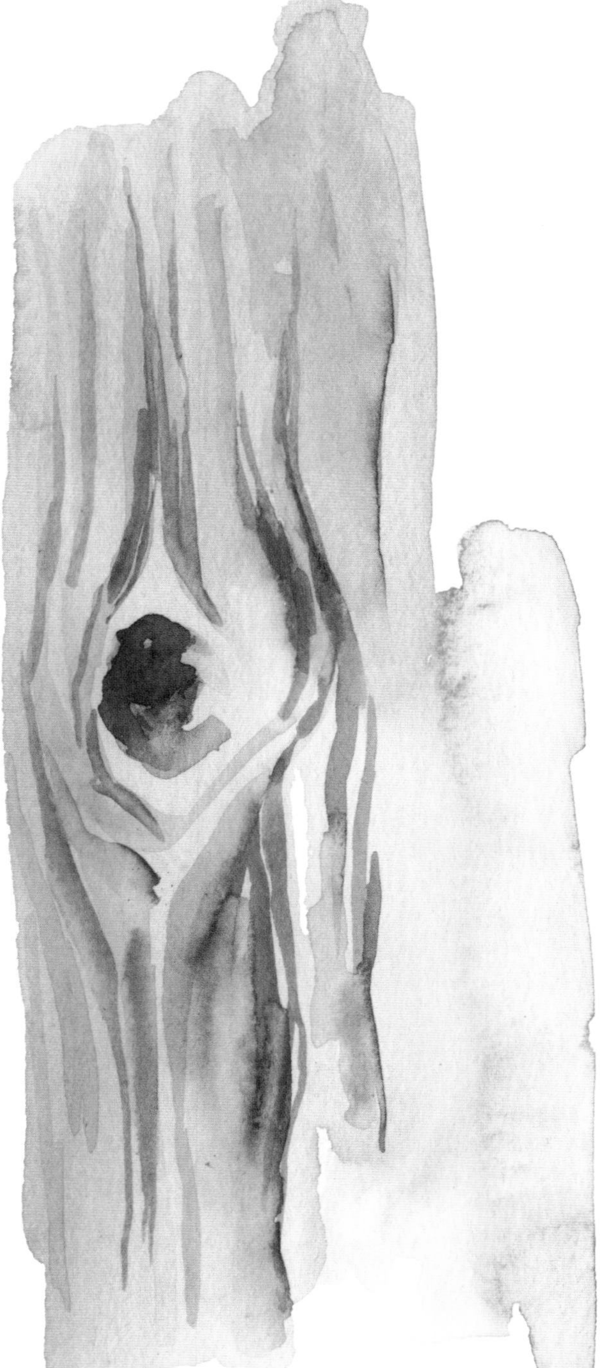

DAY 1

Jesus' Walk Powers Ours

The kinds of shoes you wear say a lot about your interests and activities—hiking, walking in snow, dressing up, running, walking on the beach—there's a shoe for every "walk" of life.

Our two legs and two feet were made for walking—they are the way most of us get from point A to point B. Sure, we have cars, trains, and planes that take us great distances today, but that is a relatively new thing. It makes sense then why the Scriptures have so much to say about how we walk.

In 1969, astronaut Neil Armstrong spoke these now-familiar words: "That's one small step for a man, one giant leap for mankind." He spoke those words as he walked on the moon! His journey, his words, and certainly his walk captured the imagination of the whole world, and he rightly understood that his stroll on the moon meant far more than just the steps he took. He walked on behalf of all mankind. You and I may never walk in such a fantastic place, but *how* and *where* we walk still matters.

Jesus, the Son of God, walked among us as one of us. He walked across His nation, Israel, for three years, teaching the way of God. He walked with 12 men whom He had chosen to carry His message, and they learned to walk as He did. Jesus' final walk was the most important walk ever taken. He walked with a wooden cross on His shoulders—a cross that He carried for us. He walked to the place His Father had determined, carrying our guilt, our shame, and the wrath we deserved for our sin. Because He took that walk, we can walk in newness of life.

The good news of the gospel is that Jesus walked the road to the cross and accomplished salvation on our behalf. It is the gospel of peace because Jesus paid the price for those who believe in Him to have no barrier to God or conflicts with Him.

The apostle Paul wrote, "Put on the whole armor of God...as shoes for your feet, having put on the readiness given by the gospel of peace" (Ephesians 6:11,15).

The shoes from the armor of God are the "readiness given by the gospel of peace"—that is, the ability to walk with the power and the peace that the good news of Jesus provides. Because Jesus walked on earth to make new life in Christ a reality, we can stand—and walk—in that newness of life. We can move differently because our shoes are powered not by the best cushioning, greatest arch technology, or sturdiest heels, but by the transforming power of the gospel of peace.

TO DWELL ON:

Jesus enables us to walk in a new way.

TO DISCUSS:

1. What are your favorite shoes to wear and why?
2. What might it look like to put on shoes of "readiness given by the gospel of peace" tomorrow morning before heading off to school, work, a playdate, or errands? Share with one another.

TO MEMORIZE:

Stand therefore, having fastened on the belt of truth, and having put on the breastplate of righteousness, and, as shoes for your feet, having put on the readiness given by the gospel of peace.

EPHESIANS 6:14-15

DAY 2

Walking the Narrow Road

Given a choice, we typically choose the shortest, easiest path to get to where we're going. We consider traffic, time of day, and construction along the routes we take. No one signs up for a bumpy, difficult, tedious journey.

But, as Christ-followers, the Bible tells us that walking with Jesus is challenging in the world in which we live. What's so hard about it, you ask? Well, for starters, it is not the way other people live. You have only to look to television, social media, or friends at school to see what I mean. Jesus said that the gate and the path that lead to life are narrow, and there are few who find it. Most people want to take the easy way, but Jesus tells us that the "easy way" leads to destruction.

Jesus often elaborated on the difficulties of walking with Him. When a rich young ruler came asking how to be saved, Jesus told him to sell everything he had (Mark 10). Jesus instructed him this way not because all of us need to sell everything to please God, but because He clearly identified what was in the young man's heart. The rich young ruler was in love with his stuff. He left Jesus sad because he didn't want to choose Jesus over his love for his wealth. Jesus went on to tell His disciples, much to their amazement, that it is easier for a camel to go through the eye of a needle (a very tight space) than for a rich man to enter God's kingdom. Yikes!

If you find the needle's eye daunting, then Jesus' words in Luke 9:23 will be equally alarming: "If anyone would come after me, let him deny himself and take up his cross daily and follow me." Not too long after Jesus spoke these words, the disciples came to understand the full meaning of "take up your cross" as they watched Jesus carry one to Calvary. Jesus meant that to walk with Him, you must choose Him instead of your self-centered ways of happiness and achievement.

Narrow gates and roads, carrying crosses, and daily dying to self—it sounds like a lot to lose. But consider Jesus' question in Luke 9:25: "What does it profit a man if he gains the whole world and loses or forfeits himself?" If we seek to save our life, Jesus warns, we will lose it. But if we lose our life for Jesus' sake, we will find it. Jesus calls us to give up our own plans and desires so that we can discover His way to *life*. Walking with Jesus isn't simply walking away from what you think will bring you happiness. It's walking *toward* what He promises will bring you joy.

TO DWELL ON:

Walking with Jesus on the narrow road is better than finding your own way on the wide road of destruction.

TO DISCUSS:

1. Describe what the wide road looks like among your peers and friends.

2. Share a time when choosing to walk with Jesus on a narrow road brought joy and freedom.

TO MEMORIZE:

Enter by the narrow gate. For the gate is wide and the way is easy that leads to destruction, and those who enter by it are many. For the gate is narrow and the way is hard that leads to life, and those who find it are few.

MATTHEW 7:13-14

DAY 3

Walk by the Spirit

Have you ever seen a marching band in action? It's quite a sight—hundreds of men and women moving in unison to music, playing their instruments, and performing orchestrated motions on cue with precision. On command, the troupe moves as one—starting, stopping, turning—each person's movements perfectly timed. It is a work of artistry—an entire group responding to their training and moving in accordance with the leader's command, delivering a performance spectacular both to watch and to hear.

As followers of Christ, we have Someone who calls out directions that we are to follow. Paul writes in his letter to the Galatians: "Since we live by the Spirit, let us keep in step with the Spirit" (5:25 NIV). There is great encouragement here! Paul is writing to the Galatians about no longer being under the Old Testament law but being free in Christ. It may not feel like freedom to obey commands and do as you're told, but listen to what the apostle Paul taught. He said that the law was given so that we might know what God expects of us. The problem was that no one could ever keep it! Not you, not me, not even your Sunday School teacher. No one under the law was ever found to be righteous except Jesus, who fulfilled it for us. Walking by the law was like a spiritual treadmill—lots of striving but getting nowhere.

God changed our hopelessness by giving us His Spirit to live by— to "keep in step with." Galatians 5:18 says, "But if you are led by the Spirit, you are not under the law." That means, when we walk in step with our Savior, we get off the treadmill of trying harder to please Him and walk *with* Him instead. As followers of Jesus, following His commands—keeping in step with Him—is not restrictive and exhausting, but freeing and empowering.

That is good news to walk in today.

TO DWELL ON:

When we trust Jesus, walking in step with the Spirit leads to freedom.

TO DISCUSS:

1. Do you like being told what to do? Why or why not?
2. Describe a time when walking in step with God's commands felt freeing.

TO MEMORIZE:

> If we live by the Spirit,
> let us also keep in step with the Spirit.
>
> GALATIANS 5:25

DAY 4
Walk by Faith

When was the last time you gave thanks for your five senses? Without sight, smell, hearing, touch, and taste, our experience of God's pleasure in creation would be limited. Can you imagine not experiencing the anticipation of cinnamon rolls in the oven? Or the sound of ocean waves crashing on the rocks? Or your mom's amazing back rubs? What if you never witnessed the pink sunset that glows after dinner? God intended for us to feel and enjoy all that He's created for us on earth and gave us all various ways to experience His creation.

But did you know there's something bigger that you can't touch, hear, see, taste, or smell? Something or someone greater than what your five senses can know on their own? As Psalm 19:1 says, "The heavens declare the glory of God, and the sky above proclaims his handiwork." We see a sunrise or a starry night with our eyes, but those sights call out something more than just their physical beauty. They declare God's greatness, and to grasp Him, we need faith. Faith is the sense that enables us to move beyond sight, smell, sound, taste, and touch.

If you try walking with your eyes closed, it will be just a matter of time before something goes badly (as in, don't try this at home.) Our eyes are vitally important for walking. In the same way, faith is our spiritual sight for walking in Christ. Paul tells the Corinthians, "We walk by faith, not by sight" (2 Corinthians 5:7). We cannot see God with our eyes, but we do "see" Him by faith. You see, you can't walk wisely with Jesus by simply keeping your physical eyes open; you must open the eyes of your heart to the Word of God.

The more we know Jesus through His Word, the more we see Him through our eyes of faith. And when we see through eyes of faith, we walk by faith. Our heavenly Father never intended for us to read the map, plot the course, and finish the race on our own strength. Instead, He wants to grow our faith so that we might trust Him for every step.

TO DWELL ON:

We were made to trust God and to walk by faith.

TO DISCUSS:

1. What does it feel like to walk in the dark?
2. Share one way you currently can't "see" how to walk, and how the Lord is teaching you to have eyes of faith as you go.

TO MEMORIZE:

> So we are always of good courage. We know that while we are at home in the body we are away from the Lord, for we walk by faith, not by sight.
>
> 2 CORINTHIANS 5:6-7

DAY 5

Walk with the Wise

Have you ever watched a relay race (or run one yourself)? A relay is when each member of the team trains individually and together, practicing and coordinating successful blind handoffs (the transferring of the baton), and strategizing for their own leg of the race. It's a race where one person's success contributes to the success of the entire team. It's an event where it matters who you run with.

We're careful to pick our teams when it comes to athletics but often careless when it comes to who we run and walk with in following Jesus. The Bible has much to say about keeping good company and walking with the wise in the book of Proverbs. One such verse is Proverbs 13:20: "Whoever walks with the wise becomes wise, but the companion of fools will suffer harm." The wisdom in this instruction isn't meant to make us unloving toward those who don't think or believe like us, but it is a reminder that it matters who you walk with because who you walk with affects how you finish the race.

"Walking" is purposefully moving toward a destination. Can you really walk *with* someone who isn't going where you're going? It would be like doing a three-legged sack race with someone who decides to go get ice cream instead of finishing the race. It'd be impossible to stay your course. Imagine, on the other hand, partnering with someone who has the same aim, sees the same goal, and works *with* you to get to the finish line. As funny as it may sound, three-legged sack races are won by pairs who hold on to each other, move in unison, and work together. We're instructed to walk with the wise because the encouragement of a friend who loves the Lord and walks wisely with Him encourages our walk as we finish the course.

And just as it is with a relay race or the three-legged sack race at the park, you must first be the teammate or partner you long to have. If you walk with Jesus on the narrow road, in the Spirit, by faith, you will be the wise friend who encourages the walk of the wise. The body of Christ—your team—is counting on you to walk wisely with the Lord.

TO DWELL ON:

Who you walk with affects your walk.

TO DISCUSS:

1. Whom do you spend the most time with? Who influences your everyday life the most?
2. Share something wise you've learned from a friend.

TO MEMORIZE:

> Whoever walks with the wise
> becomes wise, but the companion
> of fools will suffer harm.
> Proverbs 13:20

FOUNDATION 8

CULTIVATE PRAISE, PRAYER, THANKSGIVING.

*Rejoice always, pray without ceasing,
give thanks in all circumstances;
for this is the will of God in Christ Jesus for you.*

1 THESSALONIANS 5:16-18

DAY *1*
Cultivation Takes Time

"Cultivate" is a gardening term that means both to prepare the soil—to develop the land for sowing—and to care for, water, and nurture the growing plants. A veggie garden doesn't suddenly pop up in the summer with ripe tomatoes or cucumbers by accident. The only way for vegetables to grow in their season is for someone to work the soil and prepare it to produce growth. A farmer knows there is work to be done year-round if he is to have healthy crops.

The Bible has a lot to say about cultivating: "Whoever works his land will have plenty of bread, but he who follows worthless pursuits will have plenty of poverty" (Proverbs 28:19). Jesus used the picture of seeds and watering as a way to describe how salvation takes root in one's life, so cultivation isn't important just for gardening—it's important for spiritual growth as well.

Do you merely water the seeds of faith in your life on Sundays at church, or do you cultivate your life as a follower of Jesus day by day? It is hard work and takes time to plow the soil of our hearts for spiritual growth, but we don't do it alone. God works in us "to will and to work for his good pleasure" (Philippians 2:13).

The plow of prayer plants dependence upon God.
The plow of praise plants the seeds of joy and delight in God.

The plow of thanksgiving plants hope and peace, and it is powerful for killing the weeds of discontentment, bitterness, and selfishness.

A farmer goes through all the effort of preparing the soil, plowing the field, planting seeds and watering—day after day—because he knows there will be a harvest. In the same way, we must carefully nurture what God has planted in our hearts. Prayer, praise, and thanksgiving are fruits of knowing Jesus and having new life in Him. They also effectively keep our hearts fertile for the seed of God's Word. The Word, in turn, teaches us the life-giving truths of God's faithfulness, producing richer soil in which to grow. It may take time, but no part of cultivating prayer, praise, and thanksgiving goes wasted.

TO DWELL ON:

We grow in our faith when we cultivate a life of praise, prayer, and thanksgiving.

TO DISCUSS:

1. Have you ever planted a seed? What did you have to do to nurture its growth?
2. How can you plow with the tools God's given you through prayer, praise, and thanksgiving to grow your faith?

TO MEMORIZE:

> For it is God who works in you, both to will
> and to work for his good pleasure.
>
> PHILIPPIANS 2:13

DAY 2

Directing Our Praise

Everyone talks about things they are excited about. Everywhere you turn, you can see people praising what they love—sports teams, celebrities, movies, music, and hobbies. We all have our lists.

We can get excited about many things, but we were made to worship only One—Jesus Christ. He deserves our highest praise because there is nothing and no one greater than Him. But sometimes we end up praising and celebrating what God has made in this world more than we praise or celebrate the One who created all things for His glory.

The first airplane took flight in 1903. We marvel at the plane and its significant feat, but we praise the Wright brothers, who made both the plane and the amazing advance in technology. It's the creator who is most praiseworthy.

Do you find yourself more amazed by the good things God gives you or the good God He is? We must practice and direct our praise. Because we're all affected by sin, we don't praise as we ought. A line in an old hymn says, "Tune my heart to sing Thy grace." How does that tuning happen? When we seek God in the pages of His Word and prayerfully ask Him to meet us there, He does. As we encounter God, it becomes clear that nothing and no one else compares. We can then look up from our Bibles and experience more of God in the

Cultivate Praise, Prayer, Thanksgiving

world He has created because "the heavens declare the glory of God, and the sky above proclaims his handiwork" (Psalm 19:1).

God has designed the entire creation to reflect His greatness so that we might respond to Him in praise.

TO DWELL ON:

We were made to praise our Creator!

TO DISCUSS:

1. Ask someone in your family what they think your favorite thing is. What do you say about it?

2. Take inventory: Do you praise God's gifts or God Himself more? Speak praises about the Creator to one another.

TO MEMORIZE:

> The heavens declare the glory of God, and the
> sky above proclaims his handiwork.
>
> PSALM 19:1

DAY 3

The Practice of Prayer

Do you have a best friend? How often do you talk with him or her? Imagine loving and enjoying that friend and yet not spending time with him or her. Wouldn't it be difficult to know your friend better, share what's on your mind, and grow your relationship if you didn't talk to each other? That's what it's like when we don't make time to pray.

Maybe you pray before bed, when someone is sick, or at the dinner table. Praying together as a family or in community is part of what God intended for us, but God also wants us to have a *personal* practice of prayer. Prayer isn't a religious duty or a well-rehearsed set of words we say repeatedly. No, prayer is our personal communication with the God of the universe. Prayer is out of this world because the Creator, God, makes Himself available to us in a personal, intimate way through relationship and by means of prayer.

Jesus, even while being one with His Father, made time to pray. We're told that "Jesus often withdrew to lonely places and prayed" (Luke 5:16 NIV). Jesus prayed with and for others, but He also spent time alone talking personally with His Father. Why did Jesus take time to be alone with His Father through prayer? He got away to pray to be strengthened by God. Even when He knew the journey to the cross was going to be excruciating for Him, He took time in the garden to pray, crying out to His Father: "Not as I will, but as you will" (Matthew 26:39). Jesus knew the steps to take and how to trust His Father by matching His heart up with God's through prayer.

When we look at Jesus' many examples of prayer, we learn that practicing and cultivating a life of prayer prepares us for any circumstance God allows in our lives. When we meet with Him in prayer, we grow our friendship with the Lord and our trust in Him. We become of one heart. We were made to know Jesus—not to know *about* Him, but to know Him personally through prayer.

TO DWELL ON:

Prayer is talking to God and growing your relationship with Him.

TO DISCUSS:

1. Who is your best friend? How often do you to talk to him or her?

2. How would you describe your relationship with Jesus by how you talk to Him?

TO MEMORIZE:

> In the morning, Lord, you hear my voice; in the morning
> I lay my requests before you and wait expectantly.
>
> Psalm 5:3 (NIV)

DAY 4

Active Gratitude

What is your favorite holiday? Some say Thanksgiving is their favorite time of year—even more so than Christmas! With familiar smells from the kitchen and a house full of loved ones, Thanksgiving can be truly special. More than any other time of year, we gather together with friends and family, eat until we're stuffed, and share all that we are grateful for. It's easy to say thanks to God when we are gathered together with people we love and when we're visibly aware of the abundance at our tables.

But what about every other day of the year? When we're tired of doing chores? When we wish we had more friends? When we have bills to pay? The Bible is full of examples of gratitude and praise to God in and through unwanted circumstances. We learn, by example, that gratitude is practiced, actively pursued, and given because God is always good, regardless of whether we are celebrating or grieving:

- Praise the LORD. Give thanks to the LORD, for he is good; his love endures forever (Psalm 106:1 NIV).

- Give thanks in all circumstances; for this is God's will for you in Christ Jesus (1 Thessalonians 5:18 NIV).

- Let them give thanks to the LORD for his unfailing love and his wonderful deeds for mankind, for he satisfies the thirsty and fills the hungry with good things (Psalm 107:8-9 NIV).

Giving thanks is an active choice. It is a deliberate decision to consider God's goodness and to respond accordingly. In the scriptures we just read, the word "for" means "because." That's important because we don't give thanks to get more of God's goodness. We give thanks *because* of it.

TO DWELL ON:

Give thanks all the time because God is good all the time.

TO DISCUSS:

1. What are you most grateful for?

2. Jot down a word of thanks to God each hour for the next few hours (or tomorrow morning). What do you learn about giving thanks when you actively choose to do so?

TO MEMORIZE:

> Praise the LORD. Give thanks to the LORD, for
> he is good; his love endures forever.
>
> PSALM 106:1 (NIV)

DAY 5
Keep Sowing

Any farmer will tell you that some years yield great harvests, and some years are more challenging for crops. Sometimes the rain falls and the soil is just right for growth, and sometimes the farmer fights pests and drought. A true farmer knows not to judge a field according to one or two seasons, no matter how difficult. He knows to not give up.

The apostle Paul was no stranger to obstacles and difficult circumstances, but he did not let them keep him from cultivating praise, prayer, and thanksgiving. In fact, not even imprisonment could stop him from sowing truth and praise in all those around him:

> Now I want you to know, brothers and sisters, that what has happened to me has actually served to advance the gospel. As a result, it has become clear throughout the whole palace guard and to everyone else that I am in chains for Christ. And because of my chains, most of the brothers and sisters have become confident in the Lord and dare all the more to proclaim the gospel without fear (Philippians 1:12-14 NIV).

Because Paul continued to look to Christ—praising Him, praying to Him, and sharing Him with others—the seeds of faith continued to spring up through his witness in prison and throughout the region through his letters. This same Paul reminded a church in the town of Corinth that God is the Master Gardener who determines the harvest: "The point is this: whoever sows sparingly will also reap sparingly, and whoever sows bountifully will also reap bountifully" (2 Corinthians 9:6).

We cultivate prayer, praise, and thanksgiving because even though God is in charge of the growth, we are given the opportunity to be the ones who work the field. We get to put our hands to the plow and prepare room in our hearts for thanksgiving and praise. When we practice—rehearse, repeat, rest in—the truths of God's faithfulness, we sow deeply and leave the results to God.

So don't give up. Keep sowing, keep plowing, keep cultivating. "Let us not grow weary of doing good, for in due season we will reap, if we do not give up" (Galatians 6:9).

TO DWELL ON:

Don't give up on sowing truth and growing in your praise to God.

TO DISCUSS:

1. What important skill or task takes a lot of time to learn?

2. How can you personally keep sowing and keep growing in prayer, praise, and thanksgiving?

TO MEMORIZE:

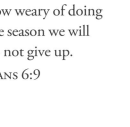

And let us not grow weary of doing good, for in due season we will reap, if we do not give up.

GALATIANS 6:9

FOUNDATION 9

BEAR WITH ONE ANOTHER

FORGIVE
as God has forgiven you.

Bearing with one another and,
if one has a complaint against another, forgiving each other;
as the Lord has forgiven you, so you also must forgive.

COLOSSIANS 3:13

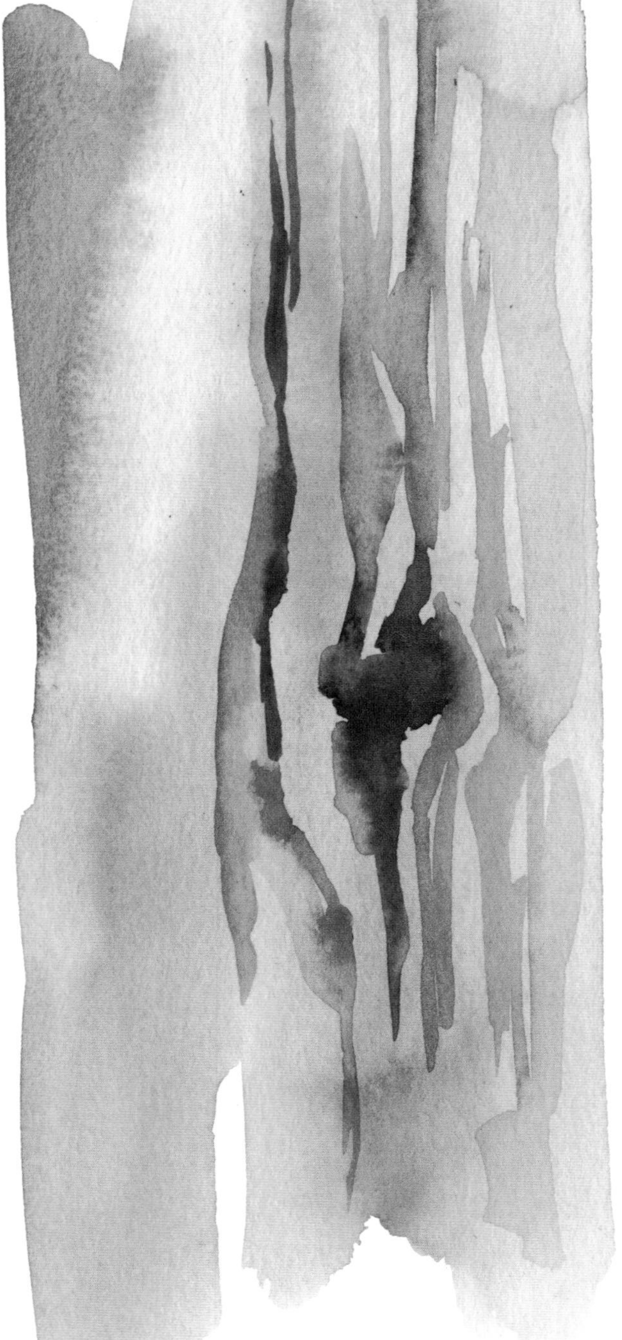

DAY *1*

As Christ Forgave You

Chances are, you've forgotten lots of things you want to remember, but remember lots of things you wish you could forget. You may have no problem recalling every detail of the way someone has hurt you. You can likely remember the tone, the words spoken, and the way you felt...and perhaps still feel. You can't unhear unkind words or undo hurtful actions. Sin and sinful actions have consequences.

It can be difficult to put forgiveness into action when you've been hurt and can't forget. But the good news of Jesus Christ is that He doesn't just help us do the difficult—He makes the impossible possible. When the apostle Paul instructed believers to "be kind to one another, tenderhearted, forgiving one another, as God in Christ forgave you" (Ephesians 4:32), he didn't suggest that we try harder to be a nicer version of ourselves. Instead, he instructed us to imitate Christ. That's what "as God in Christ forgave you" means. It means to show others what has been shown to us through Jesus.

The penalty of our sin has been forgiven and paid for by Christ on the cross. God chooses to forget our sin and not hold it against us because of His own righteousness. He says, "I, even I, am he who blots out your transgressions, for my own sake, and remembers your sins no more" (Isaiah 43:25 NIV).

We may not know how to forgive *like* Jesus, but we can forgive *because* of Jesus. It's not impossible to forgive when Jesus has already accomplished the impossible in forgiving *us* of *our* sins. We can afford to be kind, tenderhearted, and forgiving toward another because our Savior, Jesus, paid the ultimate price for our sin and the sin of those who have hurt us. Forgiveness isn't free. It cost Jesus His life. But the more you know how much you've been forgiven, the more you will freely forgive.

TO DWELL ON:

When you know how much you've been forgiven, there's nothing you can't forgive.

TO DISCUSS:

1. What have you been forgiven in Christ?
2. How does remembering your own forgiven sin change your attitude about forgiveness?

TO MEMORIZE:

Be kind to one another, tenderhearted, forgiving
one another, as God in Christ forgave you.
EPHESIANS 4:32

DAY 2

Bearing with Differences

Have you ever been tempted to think that
your life would be so much easier if everyone thought and behaved just like you? *If only
your friends saw it your way? If only your family
members came to the same conclusions you do about
things? If only others had your same measure of production, quality, or
achievement?* We may not say so, but our pride—believing ourselves
to be better or wiser than other people—causes us to be intolerant
with those who aren't up to our standards. And for prideful people,
that's usually everyone.

But God calls us as His children to be different—to be set apart:

> Therefore, as God's chosen people, holy and dearly loved,
> clothe yourselves with compassion, kindness, humility,
> gentleness and patience. Bear with each other and for-
> give one another if any of you has a grievance against
> someone. Forgive as the Lord forgave you (Colossians
> 3:12-13 NIV).

Like forgiveness, bearing with one another is possible only
because of Christ's grace toward us. Bearing with one another isn't
just a choice our mind makes to overlook and forgive an offense; it is a
continued willingness to set aside our own pride and carry the weight
of others who may not be easy to cooperate with.

In his letter to the Colossians, Paul assumes that brothers and sisters in Christ may not always think alike, act alike, or prioritize the same things in their daily lives. We are not always at the same level of spiritual maturity as other people and, because we are sinners, we struggle to be patient and tolerant.

Paul's reminder to the Colossians is that they themselves are holy and dearly loved children of God, forgiven of all that isn't up to God's standard. With that in mind, we, too, can put on humility and patience, bearing with one another when others are not yet mature, not yet wise, not yet who they need to be...knowing God is not through with them—or us—yet.

TO DWELL ON:

We can bear with our brothers and sisters in Christ because God is still at work in us.

TO DISCUSS:

1. What are some things that easily annoy you or bother you about others?

2. How does Paul's instruction to the Colossians remind you to bear with brothers and sisters in the Lord?

TO MEMORIZE:

Therefore, as God's chosen people, holy and dearly loved, clothe yourselves with compassion, kindness, humility, gentleness and patience. Bear with each other and forgive one another if any of you has a grievance against someone. Forgive as the Lord forgave you.

COLOSSIANS 3:12-13 (NIV)

DAY 3

How Many Times

Leave it to the apostle Peter to always ask
Jesus what we're secretly wondering:

> "Lord, how often will my brother sin
> against me, and I forgive him? As many
> as seven times?" Jesus said to him, "I do not say
> to you seven times, but seventy-seven times" (Matthew
> 18:21-22).

Peter, hoping to impress Jesus, suggested what seemed to be a
generous number of times to forgive someone. But Jesus answered in
such a way as to say, "Forgiveness is limitless, so stop counting."

Do you want a rule and a formula for forgiveness? Do you ever
wonder if you can take a pass on giving forgiveness for certain offenses
or when the person who hurts you doesn't repent? Maybe it seems
reasonable to say, "That's it! I've already forgiven you before, and I'm
done!" when your brother breaks something of yours for the billionth
time, when a friend hurts your feelings callously, or when your kids
lie or disobey again. Wouldn't it be so much easier to have an equa-
tion to plug your hurts and offenses into that spits out exactly what
you are supposed to say and do in response?

Instead, Jesus gives no limits to the extent of our forgiveness. He
gives no caveats for withholding forgiveness. Is there an end to God's
grace that covers our multitude of sin? Is His forgiveness toward
us bound by time, length, or depth? No, the grace of God pursues us,

Bear with One Another; Forgive as God Has Forgiven You

plucks us out of darkness, rescues us from the power of sin, and restores us again and again.

When we are tempted to keep score and to count up our generous efforts in forgiving others, remember that we can't outgive or out-forgive God. God shows us...

> All have sinned and fall short of the glory of God, and are justified by his grace as a gift, through the redemption that is in Christ Jesus (Romans 3:23-24).

Grace is the gift we can afford to give.

TO DWELL ON:

God does not limit His forgiveness of us; therefore, we should not limit our forgiveness of others.

TO DISCUSS:

1. How does it make you feel when you are repeatedly sinned against?

2. Knowing that you have done the same to God and received unlimited mercy, how can you forgive (your brother, friend, classmate) beyond measure?

TO MEMORIZE:

All have sinned and fall short of the glory of God, and are justified by his grace as a gift, through the redemption that is in Christ Jesus.

ROMANS 3:23-24

DAY 4

When It Still Hurts

Have you ever had a wound that didn't heal quickly? Or a sprain that ached even weeks after your initial injury? Sometimes wounds, especially deep wounds, can look clean, healed, and patched up on the outside but still leave a lot of pain deep inside. That's how it often is when we've been hurt in relationships. Few things ache quite like the betrayal of a friend or the consequence of a sinful offense. Even when we choose to forgive the one who hurt us, as God's Word clearly calls us to do, we can still feel the sting and hurt. Forgiveness isn't a Band-Aid, a miracle cream, or a magic wand that takes away the pain.

Unforgiveness in the heart craves vengeance with the hands. In our hurt, we want to retaliate. We might not think about physically hurting someone else, but...

- *Have you ever wanted to make fun of someone who made fun of you?*
- *Have you wanted to break something that belonged to someone who destroyed something you loved?*
- *Have you ever wanted to ruin the reputation of someone who spread lies about you?*

Forgiveness doesn't mean we have to feel good about what has been done to us, nor does it mean that sinful actions don't have

Bear with One Another; Forgive as God Has Forgiven You

consequences. It simply means that we believe that God is just. So, we leave justice for the wrongdoing to God instead of withholding forgiveness to punish it ourselves. We can choose to forgive and trust God to make things right. The Bible reminds us:

God is in charge...

> Beloved, never avenge yourselves, but leave it to the wrath of God, for it is written, "Vengeance is mine, I will repay, says the Lord" (Romans 12:19).

God will take away our hurts, once and for all:

> He will wipe away every tear from their eyes, and death shall be no more, neither shall there be mourning, nor crying, nor pain anymore, for the former things have passed away (Revelation 21:4).

TO DWELL ON:

We don't have to feel pain-free to forgive and trust God to make things right.

TO DISCUSS:

1. Have you ever had an injury that didn't heal quickly? What was it like to wait for it to heal?

2. Write a prayer to the Lord, releasing any unforgiveness toward someone who has wronged you.

TO MEMORIZE:

He will wipe away every tear from their eyes, and death shall be no more, neither shall there be mourning, nor crying, nor pain anymore, for the former things have passed away.

REVELATION 21:4

DAY 5

Goal of Forgiveness

Goals help us know where we are going, and *why*. If a family is saving their pennies for a summer vacation, they will keep the goal in mind when they're tempted to indulge now in unnecessary purchases. When a student studies for a test weeks before the exam, she has a goal in mind: to be prepared and to do well when the test arrives. When we talk about forgiveness, we must have the ultimate goal in mind.

What is the goal of forgiveness? Is it simply to heal, make amends, or get along? It certainly is all these things, but more importantly, the ultimate goal is this:

> Brothers, if anyone is caught in any transgression, you who are spiritual should restore him in a spirit of gentleness. Keep watch on yourself, lest you too be tempted. Bear one another's burdens, and so fulfill the law of Christ (Galatians 6:1-2).

The goal of forgiveness and bearing with a brother or sister in Christ, is reconciliation—the process of reuniting, coming back together, becoming friends again. Simply put, it is healing the relationship. Between believers, the goal of forgiveness is reconciliation with one another. It is to spur one another on toward becoming complete in Christ.

But sometimes we must forgive a nonbeliever—someone who is

not yet a brother or sister in the family of faith. When we forgive a nonbeliever, the goal of forgiveness is that he or she might be reconciled to God, seeing in us a picture of the forgiveness that God offers through Jesus.

You see, the end goal of all forgiveness and restoration is that we might have peace with God and with each other. When we choose to forgive and bear with one another, we get to be peacemakers. Child of God, there is no better goal for us today.

> Blessed are the peacemakers, for they will be called children of God (Matthew 5:9 NIV).

TO DWELL ON:

Forgiving is peacemaking.

TO DISCUSS:

1. Have you ever helped your siblings reconcile (stop fighting)? What did you say or do to help them reunite?

2. How can you be a peacemaker with a believer who is in your life? How can you be a peacemaker with a nonbeliever who is in your life?

TO MEMORIZE:

Blessed are the peacemakers, for they will be called children of God.
MATTHEW 5:9 (NIV)

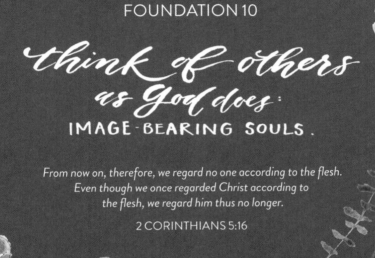

FOUNDATION 10

*think of others
as God does:*
IMAGE-BEARING SOULS.

*From now on, therefore, we regard no one according to the flesh.
Even though we once regarded Christ according to
the flesh, we regard him thus no longer.*

2 CORINTHIANS 5:16

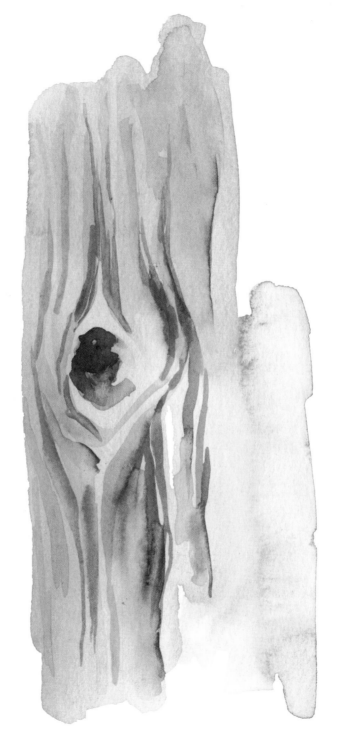

DAY *1*

Unlike the Other Animals

Going to the zoo is a bit like taking a trip around the world. Lions from Africa, tigers from Asia, and snakes from all over—just to name a few of the creatures you'll find. The zoo is a great place to learn about animals and their behaviors. Perhaps you've seen an elephant, massive as it is, nimbly pick up the smallest piece of grass with its trunk. Or maybe you've exchanged glances with a Golden Tamarin as he hangs upside down by his tail. Then there's the feeding time for the seals. It is a marvel to watch these mammals cut through the water like fur-coated torpedoes, pop up on rocks, and gobble down whole fish.

But there are some things you won't see at the zoo. You won't see a zebra praying over his meal. You won't see the meerkats decorating their cages, and you certainly won't be able to have a conversation with a camel. Only one creature does these things, and it is you. We share a lot in common with other animals because we share the same environment, but we differ in some very significant ways. God tells us in Genesis 1:27 that He made man "in his own image, in the image of God he created him; male and female he created them." No other created thing was made in God's image, and it was only humans who walked with and learned from God in the Garden of Eden.

From beginning to end, the Bible teaches that God created us and wanted to know each of us in a personal and eternal way. John's Gospel tells us: "This is eternal life, that they know you, the only true God and Jesus Christ whom you have sent" (John 17:3). Here is the

Think of Others as God Does: Image-Bearing Souls

fullness of God's plan in creating us in His image. He wanted us to know Him personally and relationally—in a way that no other creature ever could.

Though sin has marred the image of God in our lives, robbing us of the perfect fellowship humans were created to have with God the Father, Jesus' life, death, and resurrection restores that image and reunites us to God. Of all the things that we can remember about ourselves and others, nothing compares to being image-bearers, made to know and glorify God. When we view others through that lens, we begin seeing who they were always meant to be.

TO DWELL ON:

Each person is made to have a personal relationship with God.

TO DISCUSS:

1. How are human beings different from other animals?
2. How would remembering other people were created for a relationship with God change the way you treat them?

TO MEMORIZE:

> From now on, therefore, we regard no one according
> to the flesh. Even though we once regarded Christ
> according to the flesh, we regard him thus no longer.
> 2 Corinthians 5:16

DAY 2
Blinded Minds

A common story line in movies and books is that of a person we're supposed to think is a good guy who turns out to be a villain. He pretends to care for those around him and usually helps them out of a tight spot, all the while planning evil things. There is always someone who suspects that he is not who he says he is, and it is that person's job to help others see it.

This is a common plot because it is every person's story. At the very beginning of our story of origin, Adam and Eve were deceived by the serpent (Satan). He assured them that they would not die by disobeying God's command. Instead, he promised that they would benefit by becoming *like* God. Satan deceived Adam and Eve into caring more about their own image and ideas than God's. Satan uses that same lie today. Paul writes in 2 Corinthians 4:3-4:

> Even if our gospel is veiled, it is veiled to those who are perishing. In their case the god of this world has blinded the minds of the unbelievers, to keep them from seeing the light of the gospel of the glory of Christ, who is the image of God.

If a person is without Christ, he is walking in darkness. He is an image-bearing soul that is blind to his true condition. He may not be a villain. He may be a "good person" by everyone's estimation.

But if he doesn't trust in Jesus to forgive him of his sins, he is walking in blindness to God and is lost in his waywardness. People are easily duped by appearances, and we—as followers of Christ—can sometimes find ourselves tricked into believing with our eyes rather than according to the truth of God's Word. Jesus calls us to be His witnesses so that we can shine the light of the gospel to those around us. Don't be discouraged when you see people seemingly blinded by the enemy's schemes or unaware of their true need for Christ. Don't give up on them—instead, see them as God sees them: people created by God who need to be brought into the light.

TO DWELL ON:

Be the light to others who may not yet see their need for Christ.

TO DISCUSS:

1. How are some of your friends blinded into caring more about their own image than being image-bearers of God?
2. Who are some people in your life you can be a light to?

TO MEMORIZE:

> In their case the god of this world has blinded the minds of the unbelievers, to keep them from seeing the light of the gospel of the glory of Christ, who is the image of God.
>
> 2 Corinthians 4:4

DAY 3

Everyone Is Creative

When we think of creativity, we think of paints and brushes, yarn, fabric, and sewing machines. We think of dancers and musicians, woodworkers and metalsmiths. We say things such as, "I'm not very creative" if we don't think we fall into one of these categories or if we've thrown unsuccessful art and DIY projects into the trash.

But in reality, everyone is creative. *Everyone!* While not everyone enjoys scrapbooking, sculpting, or painting, every person has a God-given nature to create and express creativity. That's how we were made because that's who we reflect: "God created man in his own image, in the image of God he created him; male and female he created them" (Genesis 1:27).

God formed and made us to reflect and resonate His glory and His handiwork. We had nothing to do with His formation of the earth or the greatness of His design:

> As you do not know the path of the wind, or how the body is formed in a mother's womb, so you cannot understand the work of God, the Maker of all things (Ecclesiastes 11:5 NIV).

These reminders from Scripture (and so many more from the book of Job) make clear that God is God and we are not. The most creative, talented, or artistic person on earth has nothing on God who breathed life into man and formed him from dust. We are His divine workmanship.

Knowing this should change the way we think of ourselves and others. Rather than measure or label ourselves or others as talented, creative, not creative, or nonartistic, we can simply remember that the God who formed every person is the God who breathed infinite imagination, unique thought, and creative expression into you and me. Some use words, some use tools, some create from flour and butter. God has given each of us minds that develop ideas and creations only we can uniquely form.

TO DWELL ON:

Every person is a creative being because each person reflects a creative God.

TO DISCUSS:

1. Do you feel like a creative person? Why or why not?
2. In what way can you reflect God's creativity by being the person He's made you to be?

TO MEMORIZE:

God created man in his own image,
in the image of God he created him;
male and female he created them.

GENESIS 1:27

DAY 4

As One

Take one look at an eagle, and it's obvious it was created for flight. Anyone can recognize that a cheetah was built to run. Fish swim, monkeys swing, frogs jump, and no one is surprised because we know the connection between a creature's physical traits and the purpose of its design. No two creatures are alike, just as no two people are created the same.

Curly hair, straight hair, dark skin, freckled skin, long-legged, wheel-chaired, green-eyed, or physically blind...every man and woman God created is unique. God also gave us unique stories, backgrounds, and places to call home. Across the globe, people speak different languages and have different cultures, family traditions, and dress. A most beautiful hat to wear in one culture can seem strange in another. What tastes delicious to a family in one country would never make it to the table on the other side of the globe. The Bible tells us that, though people on the earth may look, sound, or enjoy different things from one another, they will someday be together as one if they love God:

> After this I looked, and there before me was a great multitude that no one could count, from every nation, tribe, people and language, standing before the throne and before the Lamb. They were wearing white robes and were holding palm branches in their hands (Revelation 7:9 NIV).

The beauty of God's design is that regardless of background, physical traits, language, skin color, or country of origin, each one of us bears the image of God! Doesn't that tell you something of God's creativity, heart, and purpose? God Himself does not look or sound just like one kind of people on earth. He made all of us to reflect Him.

When you meet someone who is different from you in looks, heritage, language, or physical strengths, remember that he or she may one day be a brother or sister with whom you spend all of eternity worshipping.

TO DWELL ON:

Every language, race, color, physical trait, and ethnicity will be represented in heaven.

TO DISCUSS:

1. Do you have friends from other countries? Describe the most interesting thing about their culture.

2. How does knowing you may worship in heaven next to someone completely different from you change how you treat him or her today?

TO MEMORIZE:

After this I looked, and there before me was a great multitude that no one could count, from every nation, tribe, people and language, standing before the throne and before the Lamb.

REVELATION 7:9 (NIV)

DAY 5

We Are His

Everyone tells you to be yourself.

Unfortunately, "yourself" is not always an easy thing to discern, especially in today's identity obsessed world. When asked, "Who are you?" you may be tempted to describe what you do, where you live, or what you are good at. Parents, you might think of yourself according to your job title or school degree. Kids, you might say "a soccer player" or "a swimmer." One look at social media, and you can see how obsessed we as a culture are over the issue of identity—who our friends are, what organizations we support, what pages we "like," who we know, how we look to others. Our online life becomes our identity in an age where people barely know one another face-to-face.

How do you really know exactly who you are?

It's hard to be yourself if the self you are representing is a carefully managed picture you want others to see. We weren't made to represent our "self" for our own benefit; we were made by God and for Him. As we're told in Ephesians, "We are his workmanship, created in Christ Jesus for good works, which God prepared beforehand, that we should walk in them" (Ephesians 2:10).

We are not our own. We are not the sum of our reputations, our social media pages, or what others think of us. We've been bought with a price and no longer represent ourselves, but God. As followers of Jesus, we're representatives of the work of Jesus Christ to bless others with the fruit of salvation. We were made by Him and for Him!

When we discover that our identity is in what our Savior has already done and not in what we strive to do for ourselves, the answer to the "Who am I?" question is so much easier. It's okay to be no one to everyone if you are someone to the Holy One. Being yourself is not as important as being His.

TO DWELL ON:

Our true identity is found in Jesus.

TO DISCUSS:

1. How do you typically introduce yourself when meeting someone new? How do you describe who you are?

2. What has Jesus done to make you His? How should that change your sense of identity?

TO MEMORIZE:

We are his workmanship, created in Christ Jesus for good works, which God prepared beforehand, that we should walk in them.

EPHESIANS 2:10

FOUNDATION 11

KEEP YOUR
HOPE *in* HEAVEN
and hold lightly
THE THINGS OF EARTH.

Therefore, preparing your minds for action, and being sober-minded,
set your hope fully on the grace that will be brought
to you at the revelation of Jesus Christ.

1 PETER 1:13

DAY 1
Only God

Can you imagine the shock you would feel if, while watching your favorite team play, someone from your team started passing to the other team, blocking his teammates, or even scoring against his own team? You can just imagine the outrage. Everyone would be calling for him to be kicked off the team. It is impossible to play for two teams because no one can give his full attention to two opposing sides. You can only serve one and not the other. Turns out, the same is true for people who follow Christ. First John 2:15 says, "Do not love the world or the things in the world. If anyone loves the world, the love of the Father is not in him."

God does not allow us to divide our loyalties. When He calls us to follow Him, He calls us to love and serve Him only:

> No servant can serve two masters, for either he will hate the one and love the other, or he will be devoted to the one and despise the other. You cannot serve God and money (Luke 16:13).

We cannot love both. That doesn't mean we don't enjoy the world—no, God has made the world to reflect His creativity! Psalm 19:1 says, "The heavens declare the glory of God, and the sky above proclaims his handiwork." What we cannot love are the beliefs and practices of the world. What the world values is opposed to God because it trusts in itself and not its creator.

Our love for God causes us to invest in our heavenly and eternal home, not our earthly dwelling. It causes us to declare as the psalmist did, "Better is one day in your courts than a thousand elsewhere; I would rather be a doorkeeper in the house of my God than dwell in the tents of the wicked." (Psalm 84:10 NIV). When we love God fully, everything else pales in comparison. God is right in wanting our undivided love and loyalty because He is God. But what God desires *from* us, He graciously forms *in* us as we grow in our love for Him.

TO DWELL ON:

We are called to love God only.

TO DISCUSS:

1. In what way do you feel pulled in your loyalty between God and the world?
2. Why is God worthy of your undivided loyalty?

TO MEMORIZE:

Do not love the world or the things in the world. If anyone loves the world, the love of the Father is not in him.

1 JOHN 2:15

DAY 2

Evaluate Your Treasure

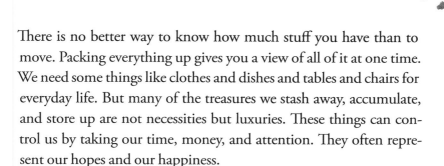

There is no better way to know how much stuff you have than to move. Packing everything up gives you a view of all of it at one time. We need some things like clothes and dishes and tables and chairs for everyday life. But many of the treasures we stash away, accumulate, and store up are not necessities but luxuries. These things can control us by taking our time, money, and attention. They often represent our hopes and our happiness.

Jesus told His followers:

> Do not lay up for yourselves treasures on earth, where moth and rust destroy and where thieves break in and steal, but lay up for yourselves treasure in heaven...For where your treasure is, there your heart will be also (Matthew 6:19-21).

The real danger of storing up earthly things is not just that they can be destroyed and stolen. The danger is that *they will steal your heart*.

It's easy to think that if we just had more of *this* or one of *those* we would be happy, but *things* never truly satisfy. We might feel secure when we have a good job and lots of money in the bank, but the fact is, it can all disappear in a moment.

How do you know if you're putting your hope in earthly possessions rather than in the things of God? You can look at the way you respond when you don't have the things you want when you want them. Are you angry, anxious, or sad?

God generously provides all that we need and even much of what we desire, but His provisions were never meant to satisfy our hearts. So loosen your grip on the things you have on earth—and set your desire on the only One who can satisfy.

TO DWELL ON:

Our earthly possessions will never satisfy us.

TO DISCUSS:

1. What are some things you are holding on to too tightly right now?
2. How is Jesus a greater treasure than anything you can possess on earth?

TO MEMORIZE:

> Where your treasure is,
> there your heart will be also.
> MATTHEW 6:21

DAY 3

Unseen Treasure

One of the most amazing discoveries from
the ancient world was the tomb of King Tut
in Egypt. Most of the tombs of the ancient
pharaohs were robbed over time, but the tomb of
King Tut was undisturbed until it was discovered in 1922.
It held amazing treasures that were supposed to go with the king into
the afterlife, but they remained in the tomb, just as they were when
he was buried. It's true—you can't take it with you.

If we live for earthly things, we will have them for a short time,
only to lose them in the end. But if we plan for eternity and use this
life to store heavenly treasure, then every day we are moving closer
to that treasure.

It can be difficult to live for something that seems far off. No one
has ever even seen the treasures of heaven, but we see the treasures of
earth every day. And we are constantly bombarded with the adver-
tisements to come and get what others have got. So how do we keep
our sights on heaven's treasure? We live by faith in God's great promises. We set our hope on all the blessings we have because of Christ.
We remember our inheritance in Christ:

> According to his great mercy, he has caused us to be
> born again to a living hope through the resurrection
> of Jesus Christ from the dead, to an inheritance that is

imperishable, undefiled, and unfading, kept in heaven for you (1 Peter 1:3-4).

Born again, living hope. Imperishable, undefiled, unfading, and *kept just for you.* This is the unseen treasure we have both now and in eternity. The Bible tells us that faith is being sure of what we hope for and certain of what we do not see (Hebrews 11:1). We can be sure of God's promises because He is good and mighty and able to make them come to pass. We can be certain of our heavenly reward because Jesus has gone ahead of us to prepare a place for us. We can treasure what we cannot see when faith keeps our eyes on Him.

TO DWELL ON:

Our true treasure is Christ and the unseen riches of our inheritance in Him.

TO DISCUSS:

1. What words do people use to describe earthly treasure? What are words you'd use to describe heavenly treasure?

2. How have your eyes of faith grown lately?

TO MEMORIZE:

Now faith is the assurance of things hoped
for, the conviction of things not seen.

Hebrews 11:1

DAY 4

Our Bodies Don't Last Forever

Have you ever looked through an old photo album and marveled at how much you and your family have changed? Photos capture a moment in time, but in real life, time just keeps on moving. The small you in the pictures may now be the big you, or the graduated you, or the married you. And however you find yourself right now, you can be sure you won't stay that way. This life will eventually come to an end as your body wears out. But what if there were a way to reverse that?

Consider what God's Word says in 1 Corinthians 15:51-52:

> Behold! I tell you a mystery. We shall not all sleep, but we shall all be changed, in a moment, in the twinkling of an eye, at the last trumpet. For the trumpet will sound, and the dead [in Christ] will be raised imperishable, and we shall be changed.

What amazing hope! Think about all we do to hold on to this life—eating well, exercising, taking medication, and even having organ transplants. Yet the truth is that no matter what we do, our bodies won't last forever. There's a difference between taking care of the body God has given us to serve Him with and obsessing over the body we don't want to fade away. One is to treasure God and the gift He's given you to serve Him with all that you have, and one is to treasure yourself and the way you look and feel above all else. We can't set our hope in heaven if we are clinging to our temporary homes (our bodies!) here on earth.

God has promised to raise us to new life and give us an imperishable body in heaven. That new body will be made for eternity and the presence of God. Everything in this life will come to an end because we are not ultimately made for an earthly life—we are made for eternity! So, don't put all your eggs in your earthly basket! Don't invest all your time, money, and energy caring for something that won't last forever. The dwelling of body and home are only meant to serve you while you're serving Him. Your soul—the unfading part of the real you—is the only thing that will last forever.

TO DWELL ON:

Take care of the part of you that will not fade when your body does.

TO DISCUSS:

1. How much time do you spend making yourself look and feel better on the outside?

2. What are some ways you can invest in your soul?

TO MEMORIZE:

> So we do not lose heart. Though our outer self is wasting away, our inner self is being renewed day by day.
>
> 2 Corinthians 4:16

DAY 5
Our True Home

What do you think of when you think of heaven? You wouldn't take a trip to somewhere you didn't research or at least hear from a friend about. If you are going on vacation, you meticulously plan out how you are going to get there, where you are going to stay, and what you are going to do while there. The more you plan, the more your excitement builds as you anticipate your time there.

Is that how we feel about heaven—are we preparing to go? For a Christ-follower, heaven is our destination. God's Word tells us a lot about heaven, and though we can't turn to pictures in the Bible to physically see heaven, there are many descriptions to help us know what to expect. Here are just a few things we can look forward to:

- Heaven is where God is.

- There will be no trace of sin in heaven. All will be made right, and God will be ours.

- Heaven is where everything is made new—no more tears, no more pain, no more broken hearts.

- Heaven will be perfect fellowship—with others and with God.

Heaven is the new and forever home we long for.

> I heard a loud voice from the throne saying, "Look! God's dwelling place is now among the people, and he

will dwell with them. They will be his people, and God himself will be with them and be their God. 'He will wipe every tear from their eyes. There will be no more death' or mourning or crying or pain, for the old order of things has passed away" (Revelation 21:3-4 NIV).

Our earthly lives are preparing us for what we will do for all of eternity. If heaven will be unending fellowship with the Lord, why would we ignore Him in our daily lives now? If heaven is filled with forever praise and adoration of God, why would we not worship Him now? If heaven will replace our temporary pain with lasting joy, why would we try to find earthly substitutes here now?

The best way to treasure heaven while on earth is to remember where you're headed...and plan accordingly.

TO DWELL ON:

Remember that heaven is your true home.

TO DISCUSS:

1. How do you prepare in advance for a special place or destination you want to go to?
2. How does remembering that heaven is your home change the way you live today?

TO MEMORIZE:

Behold, I create new heavens and a new earth, and the former things shall not be remembered or come into mind.

ISAIAH 65:17

FOUNDATION 12

STRIVE
in
GRACE.

*For it has been granted to you
that for the sake of Christ
you should not only believe in him
but also suffer for his sake.*

PHILIPPIANS 1:29

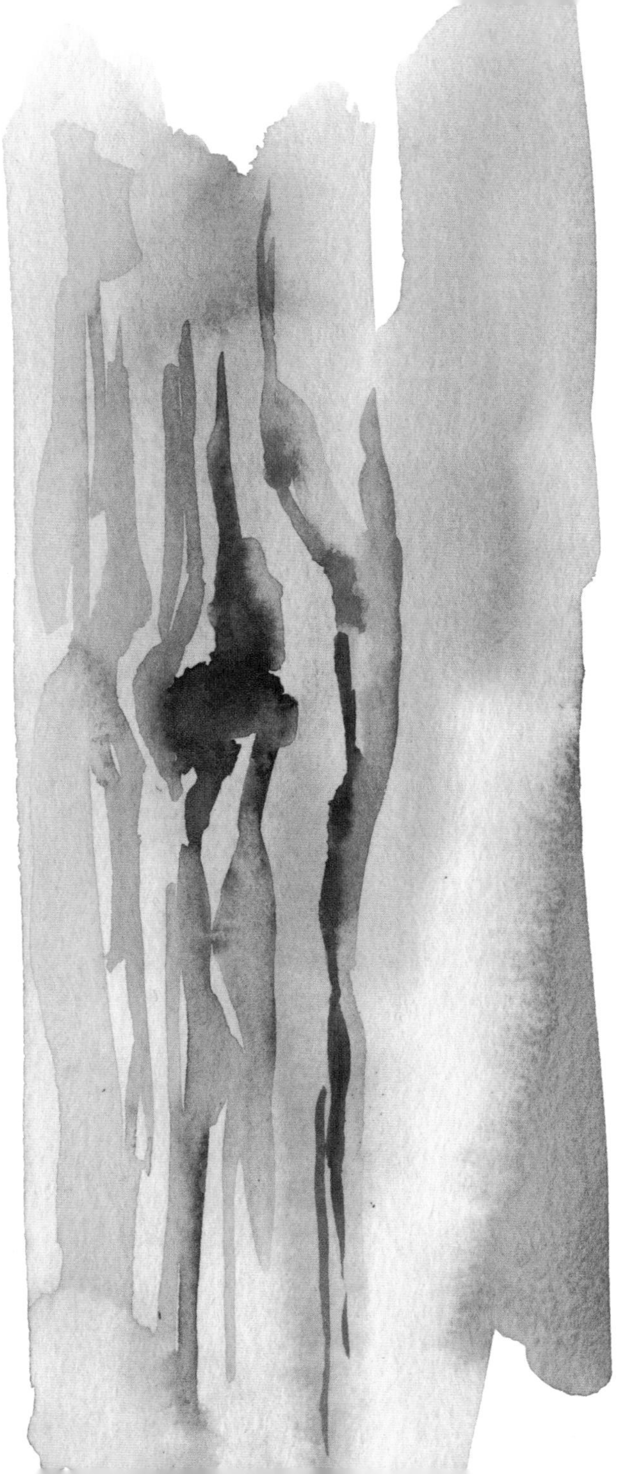

DAY 1

What You Really Need, Just in Time

Can you imagine being in the middle of the desert without any food and water only to wake up one morning and find that the ground is covered with something that tastes like a sweet cracker? That's just what happened to the Israelites after they left Egypt. They were running out of food, and God provided some for them. They called it *manna,* which means, *What is it?* What it was, was bread from heaven. God didn't stop there, either. He told Moses to strike a stone, and the next thing you know, water was pouring out! God provided for His people when they could not provide for themselves. The Israelites were powerless to save themselves out in the wilderness, but God showed Himself powerful to save. That is a picture of grace.

Grace is God's power and resources freely given to us. And because God is the creator of everything, all that we have is a gift of His grace...our very lives, our gifts and abilities, our possessions—all of it. But the most important part of God's grace is what He has done to save us from our sin and restore our relationship with Him. Paul says in Ephesians 2:8-9:

> By grace you have been saved through faith. And this is not your own doing; it is the gift of God, not a result of works, so that no one may boast.

Everything that we needed to be saved from our sin, God provided. It is not a matter of God saving us instead of us saving ourselves.

Strive in Grace

Paul says at the beginning of Ephesians 2 that we are dead in our sins until God makes us alive in Christ. That means we couldn't save ourselves if we tried.

Turns out, God's grace is more than our only option. It is the way God chooses to show us how He provides for our needs.

TO DWELL ON:

Grace is God's provision for our greatest need.

TO DISCUSS:

1. How do you think the Israelites felt when manna fell from the sky?

2. How is the grace of God (the good news of Jesus) similar to God's provision in the desert?

TO MEMORIZE:

> By grace you have been saved through faith. And this is not your own doing; it is the gift of God, not a result of works, so that no one may boast.
>
> EPHESIANS 2:8-9

DAY 2

The Try-Harder Roadblock

How would you like to swim 21 miles in frigid waters and strong currents? That is precisely what many people have done in swimming across the English Channel. It is no easy feat, but it can be done. Maybe you would like to climb a mountain so high that on the final portion of the ascent there is so little oxygen that you must return quickly to lower altitudes or face peril. It is a very dangerous journey, but it can be done.

Some people thrive on trying to do what others think is impossible. They make plans and train their bodies and minds, and sometimes they go through several failed attempts before they succeed. Even if you are not one of those people who loves to live on the edge, there is something in all of us that cheers on those who do. No one likes to be told that they can't do something. We like to think that we can always try harder.

Sometimes we try harder with God. We take God's rules, and we try to be good at them. We think that we can please God if we become a certain kind of person. *Lie less, be nicer, try not to say bad words.* When we fail at something, we redouble our efforts, thinking that we can get to a place where God is happy with us. There's just one problem: God doesn't ask us to climb the mountain of perfection because He knows we are incapable of it. God requires nothing short of absolute perfection because He is absolutely holy. God Himself is perfect and will accept nothing less than His own holy perfection. That's a mountain we can't climb. He doesn't put a mountain before us to climb by might, nor a channel to swim on our own. Instead, God carries us over the mountain and provides the boat for us to cross the sea.

Paul says in Romans 8:3-4 (NIV):

> What the law was powerless to do because it was weakened by the flesh [that's our nature], God did by sending his own Son in the likeness of sinful flesh to be a sin offering. And so he condemned sin in the flesh, in order that the righteous requirement of the law might be fully met in us, who do not live according to the flesh but according to the Spirit.

What an incredible truth! Jesus was able to accomplish what has been impossible for every other person. Jesus fulfilled God's law and the requirements for righteousness, which means that we no longer need to strive to fulfill God's law. Instead, by faith, we strive in the grace that Jesus has generously provided, that we might please Him...*His way.*

TO DWELL ON:

We cannot please God on our own, but only by His gift of grace.

TO DISCUSS:

1. What is the hardest thing you've ever tried to do (climb a mountain? hold your breath for three minutes? compete in a piano recital?)?

2. Do you struggle with trying to please God by not making mistakes? What does God's grace teach you about how to please God?

TO MEMORIZE:

What the law was powerless to do because it was weakened by the flesh, God did by sending his own Son in the likeness of sinful flesh to be a sin offering.

ROMANS 8:3 (NIV)

DAY 3
An Audience of One

Be honest: Do you clean your room, study for a test, or stay on task better when a teacher or parent is in the room? When you know you'll be graded? When your friends are watching? The truth is, most of us are more motivated to do a good job for the approval of others than for the satisfaction of a job well done.

The apostle Paul understood our human tendency to strive *for praise* rather than strive *in grace*. He writes in Colossians 3:23-24:

> Whatever you do, work heartily, as for the Lord and not for men, knowing that from the Lord you will receive the inheritance as your reward. You are serving the Lord Christ.

"Whatever you do," Paul says. Not just spiritual things or professional things. "Whatever" includes washing dishes, mowing the lawn, putting away laundry. It includes Bible reading, running a business, practicing sports, or filing your taxes. We are to do *all things* diligently—with our best effort—for a reward.

Wait—*for a reward?* That doesn't sound right! What is this reward Paul speaks of? It's our inheritance in Christ—the joy and satisfaction of being forever in the presence of Jesus! Paul says, "Yes! Do it for the reward! The reward of honoring and serving your Savior!" Unlike approval, applause, and brownie points, all of which are temporary, our inheritance in Christ—the grace of God—is an eternal, unfading, unending reward.

So, do a good job, be diligent, follow through, and keep your promises. Work hard, and don't be lazy...strive to do your best because you are serving Christ. He is reward enough for now and forevermore.

TO DWELL ON:

Work diligently for an audience of One.

TO DISCUSS:

1. What is the best reward or prize you've received for a job well done?
2. Do you work harder when your teacher (or parent, coach, boss, friend) is watching? Why?

TO MEMORIZE:

Whatever you do, work heartily, as for the Lord and not for men, knowing that from the Lord you will receive the inheritance as your reward. You are serving the Lord Christ.

Colossians 3:23-24

DAY 4

Where to Aim

To be a skilled archer, you need more than a bow and a set of arrows. You need a target. Striving to be a good bowman will get you nowhere if there's nothing to aim for. And an archer must consider speed, distance, and accuracy in light of the target. We can work hard in our walk with Jesus, but unless we know what our target is, our efforts will be in vain.

Perhaps that's why Paul ends one of his letters to the Corinthians this way:

> Finally, brothers, rejoice. Aim for restoration, comfort one another, agree with one another, live in peace; and the God of love and peace will be with you (2 Corinthians 13:11).

Paul tells his readers where to aim their efforts—what to strive for. He encourages them to make unity and reconciliation their goal and to restore what is broken. How? By rejoicing in the grace that has been given them through salvation in Jesus.

He forgave our sins. *We can forgive others.*
He restored us to Himself. *We can be reconciled to others.*
He comforts us in our pain. *We can do the same for one another.*
He made Himself to be peace. *We can be a conduit of His peace.*

You see, our efforts are in vain if we are not aiming to restore, comfort, and live in peace with other people through the joy and love of

Christ. And don't look too far. Your target may be right at home—with your mom and dad, with your kids, with your siblings, or with the extended family and friends that God has placed in your life.

Because we've been given the grace of God, we can strive for unity with brothers and sisters in that grace and not miss our mark.

TO DWELL ON:

By the grace of God, aim for restoration, unity, and peace with those around you.

TO DISCUSS:

1. Describe a recent conflict or argument you had with someone. What were you arguing about?

2. How does being happy in Jesus change the way you think of others with whom you might not agree?

TO MEMORIZE:

Finally, brothers, rejoice. Aim for restoration, comfort one another, agree with one another, live in peace; and the God of love and peace will be with you.

2 CORINTHIANS 13:11

DAY 5
Endgame

In time, we will see each person in our family grow taller, wider, older, wiser, and sometimes a little slower physically. But God has so much more than physical development in mind when He calls us to "be transformed by the renewing of your mind" (Romans 12:2 NIV).

What is the goal of striving for family core values or keeping resolutions in our walk as believers? Is it to have well-behaved children? Responsible parents? Nice families that have nice values? All those things are good by-products of striving in grace, but they are not the main reasons. As we complete this journey through these 12 foundational truths to anchor our family, we turn to the apostle Paul's stated goal:

> Him we proclaim, warning everyone and teaching everyone with all wisdom, that we may present everyone mature in Christ. For this I toil, struggling with all his energy that he powerfully works within me (Colossians 1:28-29).

To present everyone mature in Christ. Not just anyone, but the very people in *this* family—in this community God gave us—mature in Christ. That's why we continue in the truths we believe from God's Word. Paul recognizes that perseverance isn't easy, nor is maturing in Christ. It requires proclaiming Christ continually, exhorting and warning in truth, and working with fervor, powered by the Spirit, even when we feel weak. God's faithfulness supplies the energy to persevere, God's wisdom supplies the fuel for our perseverance, and God's people (us!) supply the hands and feet that take the good news of transformation in Christ to each person we do life with.

We can collect trophies, badges, or ribbons for all the finish lines we cross in our jobs, our academics, and our personal hobbies and pursuits, but the most important finish line we aim for is that of becoming *mature in Christ*. There, we present ourselves to the Father as ones who set our lives on foundational, unchanging truths—truths that shape both heart and home, the way we live and love, and how we run our race. Until that day comes, we trust Him to do the work in us as we continue to strive in grace.

TO DWELL ON:

God gives us what we need to persevere and become mature in Christ.

TO DISCUSS:

1. How much have you grown in height, weight, or shoe size in the past year?
2. How much have you grown in maturity, wisdom, and love for God in the past year?

TO MEMORIZE:

> Him we proclaim, warning everyone and
> teaching everyone with all wisdom, that
> we may present everyone mature in Christ.
> For this I toil, struggling with all his energy
> that he powerfully works within me.
> COLOSSIANS 1:28-29

From our family to yours

—The Simons Family

About the Authors

RUTH CHOU SIMONS is a bestselling and award-winning author, artist, entrepreneur, and speaker, using each of these platforms to spiritually sow the Word of God into people's hearts. Through her online shoppe at GraceLaced.com and her social media community of hundreds of thousands, Simons shares her journey of God's grace intersecting daily life with word and art. Ruth and her husband, Troy, are grateful parents to six boys and reside in the mountains of Western Colorado

TROY SIMONS spent two decades investing in full-time pastoral ministry, preaching, church-planting, and co-founding a classical school. He now works alongside Ruth as COO of GraceLaced. Raising their six boys is their greatest adventure.

Connect with Us:

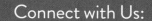 ruthchousimons

 troydsimons

Share your thoughts and
join the conversation by using the hashtag:
#OurFamilyFoundations
#FoundationsBook

Find more resources...
from Ruth and Troy at RUTHANDTROY.COM
from Ruth at RUTHCHOUSIMONS.COM

Find art prints of the 12 biblical truths from this book,
and more inspirational art by Ruth Chou Simons, at
GRACELACED.COM.

Other books available from

RUTH CHOU SIMONS